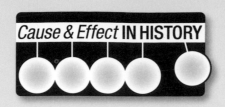

Cause & Effect IN HISTORY

Cause & Effect:
The September 11
Attacks

Robert Green

ReferencePoint
Press®

San Diego, CA

© 2016 ReferencePoint Press, Inc.
Printed in the United States

For more information, contact:
ReferencePoint Press, Inc.
PO Box 27779
San Diego, CA 92198
www.ReferencePointPress.com

LIBRARY OF CONGRESS CATALOGING-IN-PUBLICATION DATA

Green, Robert, 1969-
  Cause & effect : the September 11 attacks / by Robert Green.
    pages cm. -- (Cause & effect in history)
  Includes bibliographical references and index.
  Audience: Grade 9 to 12.
  ISBN-13: 978-1-60152-788-2 (hardback)
  ISBN-10: 1-60152-788-8 (hardback)
1. September 11 Terrorist Attacks, 2001--Juvenile literature. 2. September 11 Terrorist Attacks, 2001--Influence--Juvenile literature. I. Title. II. Title: September 11 attacks.
  HV6432.7.G718 2015
  973.931--dc23

                                                                              2014040438

CONTENTS

"History is a complex study of the many causes that have influenced happenings of the past and the complicated effects of those varied causes."

—William & Mary School of Education,
Center for Gifted Education

Understanding the causes and effects of historical events is rarely simple. The fall of Rome, for instance, had many causes. The onslaught of barbarians from the north, the weakening of Rome's economic and military foundations, and internal disunity are often cited as contributing to Rome's collapse. Yet even when historians generally agree on a primary cause (in this instance, the barbarian invasions) leading to a specific outcome (that is, Rome's fall), they also agree that other conditions at the time influenced the course of those events. Under different conditions, the effect might have been something else altogether.

The value of analyzing cause and effect in history, therefore, is not necessarily to identify a single cause for a singular event. The real value lies in gaining a greater understanding of history as a whole and being able to recognize the many factors that give shape and direction to historic events. As outlined by the National Center for History in the Schools at the University of California–Los Angeles, these factors include "the importance of the individual in history . . . the influence of ideas, human interests, and beliefs; and . . . the role of chance, the accidental and the irrational."

ReferencePoint's Cause & Effect in History series examines major historic events by focusing on specific causes and consequences. For instance, in *Cause & Effect: The French Revolution*, a chapter explores how inequality led to the revolution. And in *Cause & Effect: The American Revolution*, one chapter delves into this question: "How did assistance from France help the American cause?" Every book in the series includes thoughtful discussion of questions like these—supported by facts, examples, and a mix of fully documented primary and secondary source quotes. Each title also includes an overview of the event so that readers have a broad context for understanding the more detailed discussions of specific causes and their effects.

The value of such study is not limited to the classroom; it can also be applied to many areas of contemporary life. The ability to analyze and interpret history's causes and consequences is a form of critical thinking. Critical thinking is crucial in many professions, ranging from law enforcement to science. Critical thinking is also essential for developing an educated citizenry that fully understands the rights and obligations of living in a free society. The ability to sift through and analyze complex processes and events and identify their possible outcomes enables people in that society to make important decisions.

The *Cause & Effect in History* series has two primary goals. One is to help students think more critically about history and develop a true understanding of its complexities. The other is to help build a foundation for those students to become fully participating members of the society in which they live.

IMPORTANT EVENTS RELATED TO THE SEPTEMBER 11 TERRORIST ATTACKS

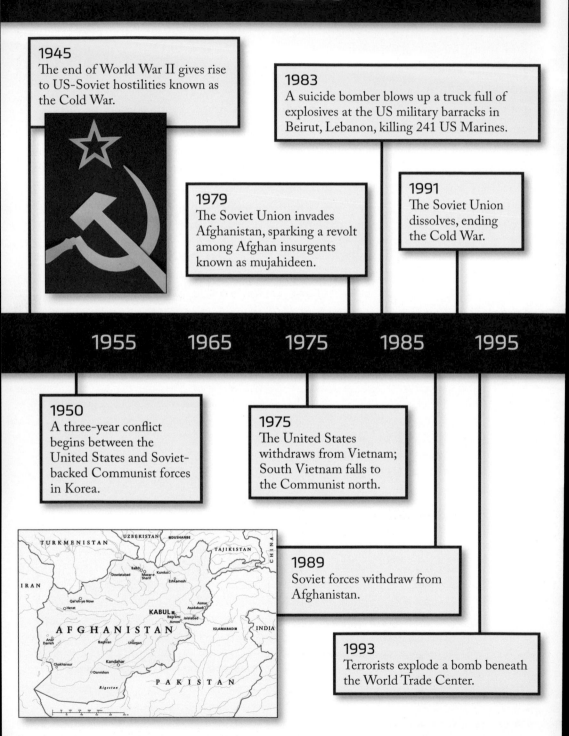

1945
The end of World War II gives rise to US-Soviet hostilities known as the Cold War.

1983
A suicide bomber blows up a truck full of explosives at the US military barracks in Beirut, Lebanon, killing 241 US Marines.

1979
The Soviet Union invades Afghanistan, sparking a revolt among Afghan insurgents known as mujahideen.

1991
The Soviet Union dissolves, ending the Cold War.

1955   1965   1975   1985   1995

1950
A three-year conflict begins between the United States and Soviet-backed Communist forces in Korea.

1975
The United States withdraws from Vietnam; South Vietnam falls to the Communist north.

1989
Soviet forces withdraw from Afghanistan.

1993
Terrorists explode a bomb beneath the World Trade Center.

1996
Osama bin Laden declares war against the United States.

1998
US embassies in Kenya and Tanzania are bombed by terrorists.

2003
The United States invades Iraq and topples the government of Saddam Hussein.

2004
The United States begins using unmanned drones to attack Taliban and al Qaeda targets in Pakistan.

2014
The United States bombs militants from the Islamic State, an al Qaeda offshoot, when they enter Iraq.

2005
Al Qaeda bombs three American hotels in Amman, Jordan.

2000   **2005**   **2010**   **2015**   **2020**

2001
Terrorists attack US targets on September 11; the United States invades Afghanistan.

2011
US Special Forces track down and kill Osama bin Laden in Pakistan; US troops withdraw from Iraq.

2000
While refueling in Yemen the USS *Cole*, an American warship, is rammed by a boat carrying explosives.

Understanding the Unthinkable

While the devastating attacks that visited American shores on September 11, 2001, can be chronicled in precise detail, understanding why the attacks happened presents a challenge. In the days just after September 11, Americans reacted with disbelief. The attacks seemed to have no clear causes and led to unthinkable consequences. They resulted in thousands of civilian deaths, a general rise in fear, and military campaigns that are continuing to this day.

While the dust of these events has not yet settled, historians have tried to put the attacks into a historical context. Often, this is done by comparing the September 11 attacks with earlier historical events. The first event that springs to mind is the only other major attack on US soil in the twentieth century—the Japanese surprise attack on Pearl Harbor, Hawaii, on December 7, 1941. The attack killed more than twenty-four hundred Americans as dive bombers emerged out of the tranquil skies above the island of Oahu and smashed the US Pacific Fleet. The attack drew the United States into World War II and prompted US president Franklin Delano Roosevelt to describe December 7 as "a date that will live in infamy."[1]

There are some clear parallels between the September 11 terrorist attacks and the Japanese attack on Pearl Harbor. Both attacks arrived from the skies above unexpectedly, on sunny, clear days. Both wrought terrific death and destruction that shocked Americans. And both prompted the United States to launch protracted military campaigns with the specific purpose of preventing the enemy from ever repeating the attacks on American territory. And indeed, both dates will forever live in infamy.

A Search for Precedents

Despite the similarities, however, much was different about the attacks, too. The destruction wrought by the Japanese attack occurred at a naval base far from the routine life of America's cities. Finding a historical precedent for an attack on a major American city requires a look at an even earlier conflict in American history.

In the War of 1812, which actually lasted for two and a half years, the recently established United States declared war on the United Kingdom to prevent interference with its shipping and to end British meddling in US territory. The battles were fought at sea and on US soil. It was, in fact, the last US war against a foreign power fought on the American mainland, and the fighting resulted in some symbolic defeats for the United States. In August 1814, for example, British troops sacked Washington, DC, the nation's capital, and burned the White House and the Capitol Building.

After being struck by hijacked airliners on September 11, 2001, the World Trade Center's North Tower pours forth black smoke as the South Tower bursts into flames. The causes and consequences of these attacks are still unfolding.

Not until the September 11 attacks would such symbolic targets again come under attack. "There's a macabre symmetry," writes historian John Lewis Gaddis, comparing the War of 1812 with the September 11 attacks, "in the possibility that the fourth plane hijacked on September 11—which crashed presumably after an uprising among the passengers—probably had one of these buildings as its target."[2]

Neither Pearl Harbor nor the British sacking of Washington, however, presents a perfect historical precedent for understanding the events of September 11, 2001. Both attacks involved the armed forces of sovereign nations fighting in a conventional manner. This was how wars were traditionally fought—between the armies of nations in conflict, with soldiers flying their national flag and wearing the insignia of their nation's armed forces.

Terrorist organizations, by contrast, seek to blend in. Their plots require the cultivation of normalcy to avoid detection. Moreover, terrorist groups, such as those who attacked the United States, attract followers from different nations and operate from scattered and secretive locations. Perhaps the only historical precedent for fighting this kind of stateless enemy was the Barbary Wars, which lasted for the first decade and a half of the nineteenth century.

The Barbary pirates provoked the United States into war by preying on civilian shipping in the Mediterranean Sea. "In response, the United States launched the Barbary wars," explain security experts Gal Luft and Anne Korin, "the first successful effort by the young republic to protect its citizens from a ruthless, unconventional enemy by fighting a protracted struggle overseas."[3]

Turning the Ordinary into the Terrible

While historians sifted through the past to help explain the September 11 attacks, Americans continued to believe that something was truly new. The terrorist attacks were so sudden and so unimaginable that they created an anxiety different from that of previous conflicts. And in previous wars there was generally a clear beginning and a clear end. The events before September 11 can help explain the rise of terrorism, but it is unknown whether the war against terror will ever have an ending as clearly marked as wars of the past. This is war against a fundamentally different kind of enemy.

"If the world today is far safer than it was only a few decades ago, and generally more peaceful than it has ever been in human history, then why don't we feel safer than we do?" asks author Michael Lind. "Partly it is because of the continuing genuine threat of terrorist incidents like the Boston [Marathon] bombing, which are unnerving because they can happen in places like our own neighborhoods."[4]

The anxiety created by terrorist attacks is so acute because they arrive, unlike conventional wars, with little warning. Indeed, these attacks seek to unnerve the general population by making use of unconventional weapons and by attacking where least expected. "What was striking about September 11 was the success with which the terrorists transformed objects we had never before regarded as dangerous into weapons of lethal potency," writes Gaddis. "There was nothing exotic here like bombs or even firearms. They used instead the objects of everyday life: pocket knives, twine, box-cutters and, of course, commercial aircraft."[5]

> "What was striking about September 11 was the success with which the terrorists transformed objects we had never before regarded as dangerous into weapons of lethal potency."[5]
>
> —Historian John Lewis Gaddis.

It was simply unthinkable for most Americans that such an attack could appear suddenly from the blue skies on a sunny autumn day and cause such loss of life and the destruction of American landmarks. But understanding the unthinkable becomes even more important in a world still living with the threat of terrorism.

CHAPTER ONE

A Brief History of the September 11 Attacks

When flight attendant Betty Ong contacted American Airlines on the morning of September 11, 2001, Flight 11 was already in a state of chaos. Air traffic control, which manages flights criss-crossing the skies above the United States, had already lost contact with the plane. An air traffic controller had been telling the plane to gain altitude for at least six minutes with no response by the time Ong reached an airline representative from a phone in the plane's rear galley. She reported that the cockpit had been breached by attackers wielding knives. The five attackers had stabbed the flight attendants, stormed the cockpit, and forced the passengers toward the back of the plane. "I think we are getting hijacked,"[6] Ong reported.

That fear was confirmed moments later when an air traffic controller in Boston picked up a voice from the cockpit of Flight 11. "We have some planes," the voice said. "Just be quiet and it will be O.K."[7] The voice was later identified as that of Mohamed Atta, an Egyptian national who had taken flying lessons in Florida in the months preceding the attacks. Now he was at the controls of Flight 11, and his words gave one of the first indications that the day was only going to get worse. As Atta's words implied, it was not only Flight 11 that was under attack. In total, four planes were hijacked on the morning of September 11, 2001. Two flights originated in Boston and were scheduled to land in Los Angeles. Hijackers also took control of a flight heading from Washington, DC, to Los Angeles and a flight from Newark, NJ, en route to San Francisco.

They chose the cross-continental flights because they knew that the planes would be fully loaded with jet fuel to propel them across

> "We have some planes. Just be quiet and it will be O.K."[7]
>
> —Mohamed Atta, hijacker of Flight 11.

the country. The highly combustible fuel turned the planes into flying bombs, now controlled by terrorists who were piloting them over the eastern United States. Between about 8 a.m., when the first plane took off, and 10 a.m., when the last plane crashed, the United States experienced the worst terrorist attack in its history.

A hijacking—the seizure of a plane by passengers—is among the most feared scenarios faced by aircrews. But unlike other hijackings in history, the hijackers made no political demands and sought no safe passage to a different destination. The hijackers on September 11 were determined only to sow fear into American life. Their goal was terror, and hijacking the planes was just the first step in an elaborate plan to strike at some of America's most powerful symbols.

The first two planes hijacked that day targeted the two tallest towers of the World Trade Center in New York City. The third plane was headed to the Pentagon, the nerve center of the US military. And the final plane, which never reached its target, is believed to have been

The Pentagon, the heart of America's military, smolders after a hijacked airliner plowed into the building on September 11, 2001. The attack killed a total of 189 people.

heading for either the White House—the home and office of the president—or the Capitol Building, where the elected representatives of the people make US law.

The World Trade Center

The World Trade Center was a giant office complex in lower Manhattan, the island at the center of New York City, and it dominated the New York City skyline. The centerpieces of the office complex were

Portrait of a Terrorist

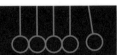

Before he piloted Flight 11 into the World Trade Center, Mohamed Atta had prepared for a career as a builder. The son of a successful lawyer and a doting mother, Atta excelled at his studies. He moved from his hometown in Egypt's Nile Delta to Cairo, the capital, to study engineering. After graduating from college he worked for a German company and eventually traveled to Hamburg, Germany, to study urban planning.

Atta, however, grew increasingly angry. He was frustrated by the corruption in the Egyptian government. Open political opposition was dangerous in Egypt. The jails were full of people who opposed the government. Resistance tended to grow within religious societies and mosques. Islam, the religion of most Egyptians, provided a moral cloak for the angry and alienated. In Germany religion became a refuge for Atta—a place where he could find comfort in a foreign land.

Fouad Ajami, a noted Middle East scholar, argues that religion was not what made Atta into a terrorist. Ajami credits a much larger historical narrative, one that brought traditional Middle Eastern life into conflict with the modern West. He points out that Atta and other young Arab men were both tempted and repulsed by the Western world. He describes them as "nowhere" men, caught between the past and present, between the Middle East and the West. Atta was unable to reconcile the traditional world of his youth with the strange openness of life abroad. "He was born," Ajami argues, "of his country's struggle to reconcile modernity with tradition."

Fouad Ajami, "Nowhere Man," *New York Times Magazine*, October 7, 2001. www.nytimes.com.

the two 110-story gleaming towers constructed of steel, concrete, and glass. Every day up to fifty thousand office workers busied themselves in the structures, and another forty thousand people passed through the sprawling complex that included an underground mall and a subway stop. The two imposing towers stood over Manhattan like the legs of a giant colossus. The Twin Towers, as they were known, were a symbol of the strength of the American economy, the largest in the world.

Atta had informed air traffic control that he was returning the plane to Boston, but as the minutes passed it became clear that he was descending into New York. Just forty-five minutes after the plane departed from Boston it slammed into 1 World Trade Center, also known as the North Tower. The plane sliced through the building between floors ninety-three and ninety-nine, toward the upper end of the structure. Ong, the rest of the flight crew, and all passengers were killed along with countless others who were in the way of the impact. The initial explosion inside the building sent a wave of fire racing through elevator shafts, blowing out elevator doors as far down as the mezzanine level near the base of the tower. The burning jet fuel then began to engulf the impacted floors. Plumes of smoke rose from the top of the building and began to fill stairways and offices inside.

> "As I left, I stopped and stared at the flames and smoke pouring from the top of the tower."[8]
>
> —BBC reporter who evacuated the World Trade Center.

The situation in the tower became chaotic. The plane had knocked out lights on some floors and in some cases interfered with the intercom system used to give instructions to office workers during an emergency. It had also severed the stairwells from the ninety-second floor, trapping workers who were above the impact zone. In the confusion most workers took it upon themselves to start evacuating the building, streaming down floor after floor of staircases. "A film of smoke descended on the plaza," writes a reporter for the British Broadcasting Corporation who was in the lobby when the plane struck. "As I left, I stopped and stared at the flames and smoke pouring from the top of the tower."[8]

The emergency response that day was like nothing New York had ever witnessed. Building personnel and police from the Port Authority, which owned the complex, began to evacuate terrified office workers, climbing floor-by-floor toward the fire above. Personnel from the fire department and police department arrived at the scene within minutes. Setting up mobile command centers, they began to clear the streets surrounding the tightly packed buildings of lower Manhattan so that fire trucks and ambulances could pass through. They too began to climb the building, searching for survivors and evacuating unharmed workers. And then the second plane hit.

United Airlines Flight 175 struck 2 World Trade Center, or the South Tower, just seventeen minutes after the North Tower was struck. When the first tower was struck many workers in the South Tower began to evacuate. Others stayed put, uncertain of what to do. Flight 175 ripped into the South Tower between floors seventy-seven and eighty-five. The second impact dispelled all thoughts of the first being an accident. Two of the most iconic buildings in the United States had just been deliberately attacked by hijackers conducting suicide missions with passenger planes.

For an hour after the impact of the second plane, rescue efforts continued in both buildings. Fires raged in both towers. Hundreds of fire fighters, police, and rescue workers—known collectively as first responders—combed the buildings for survivors and helped people make the long descent to safety. Office workers on the floors above the impact zone of the initial crashes were for the most part trapped. Frantic calls for assistance flooded emergency lines. Records of the 911 calls coming from trapped workers captured the desperation of the situation. "Trade Center again," an operator relayed to a dispatcher, "88th and 89th floor. Smoke conditions trapped."[9]

While thousands of workers in the buildings had been evacuated, the situation was growing worse for those stuck inside. Fire was raging on the upper floors. Trapped workers attempted to make their way to the roofs. Police helicopters attempted to land on the roofs but the fire and smoke drove them back. Parts of the damaged and burning buildings had been falling since the initial impact of the planes, making it unsafe for the army of rescue workers near the base of the towers. Then, the unthinkable happened.

At a minute before 10 a.m. the top floors of the South Tower began to give way. As the top of the building came down, the weight caused floor after floor to collapse like horizontal dominoes. Ten seconds later the building was a smoldering pile of rubble. The ash and dust kicked up by the collapse blanketed people around the site as they scurried away. Rescue workers in the North Tower reported feeling a thunderous vibration like an earthquake.

Orders were given to evacuate immediately. Some rescuers refused to leave until they had finished clearing the building. Others never got the order and kept searching for survivors. At 10:28 a.m. the North Tower followed suit, rumbling downward and killing all but sixteen people left inside.

Recollections of September 11 will often begin with a description of the beautiful weather. Bright early autumn sunlight and clear skies

A series of photographs (top, left to right) shows a hijacked airliner as it approaches and then crashes into the World Trade Center's South Tower, igniting a fireball and raining debris on the street below. Smoke billows from a gaping hole in the North Tower, which was hit minutes earlier. In the lower photographs (left to right), flames and black smoke nearly obscure the sight of the South Tower collapsing.

How Josephine Harris Saved Ladder Company 6

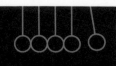

Moments after the collapse of the South Tower, firefighters from Ladder Company 6, based in New York's Chinatown, decided to evacuate the North Tower. If the South Tower had collapsed, they reasoned, the North Tower was probably next. As they raced down Stairwell B they encountered Josephine Harris, a fifty-nine-year-old bookkeeper who was resting after walking fifty floors down. She had a bad leg and was too exhausted to go on.

The firefighters scooped her up and started moving slowly downward while the clock ticked. When they reached the fifth floor Harris was too exhausted to go on. She pleaded with the firefighters to leave her, and then the building began to crumble. In less than ten seconds the 110-story building collapsed. Almost nothing remained from the surface, but somehow sixteen people had survived in Stairwell B, known afterward as the "survivors' staircase." The buried firefighters of Ladder Company 6 eventually reached the surface by radio. When they emerged from the rubble sometime later, the rescuers could not believe their eyes.

Stairwell B had collapsed above and below where the survivors were trapped. Had they descended faster or slower, they would likely not have survived. The firemen later presented Harris with a jacket inscribed with the words "Our Guardian Angel."

resulted in remarkable visibility. It was a warm early fall day, with just a hint of the cold to come. By 10:30 a.m., however, the skies over New York City were blackened with smoke and dust. New Yorkers and TV viewers all over the world watched in disbelief as the mighty buildings came crashing down. The World Trade Center had vanished from the skyline.

Terror Heads to Washington

By targeting the World Trade Center the hijackers were striking at the financial capital of the United States, New York City. But even as the twin towers of the World Trade Center were burning, two other teams of hijackers were targeting the nation's capital, Washington, DC. While New York City is the center of commercial life in the United States, Washington, DC, is the nation's political hub, the location of the federal government.

Washington's government buildings rise majestically in a neoclassical style echoing the ancient power of Greece and Rome. The three branches of the US federal government—the executive, judicial, and legislative—are all located in the humid city by the Potomac River. Just across the Potomac from the capital sits the headquarters of the US Department of Defense. Known as the Pentagon because of its five-sided layout, the headquarters of the Department of Defense is the command center of America's military might.

At 9:37 a.m. a third hijacked plane, American Airlines Flight 77, slammed into the western side of the sprawling five-story building. All 64 people on the airplane were killed, and 125 more people died from the impact of the plane ramming into the building. More than 100 others were injured. The low-slung nature of the building prevented the horrors of workers being trapped on higher floors, and responders were able to move personnel quickly away from the danger. Although the disaster was overshadowed by the collapse of the World Trade Center in New York, it would have been the most serious attack on the United States by foreign terrorists had no other attacks occurred that day.

By the time of the attack on the Pentagon, the US government was fully awakened to the fact that America was under attack. About twenty minutes after it was discovered that Flight 11 out of Boston had been hijacked, fighter jets were ordered to search for the plane. Within seconds of their takeoff from Cape Cod, Massachusetts, Flight 11 crashed into the World Trade Center. As reports came in that more flights had been hijacked, the Federal Aviation Administration—the government agency in charge of regulating air traffic—ordered all flights grounded.

US president George W. Bush was away from the White House when Flight 77 struck the Pentagon. He later took flight in Air Force One, the president's personal plane, and was dissuaded from returning to the White House since planes were still in the air. The fourth and final hijacked plane, United Airlines Flight 93, was also reported hijacked. Although it was scheduled to land in San Francisco, it had looped around and was heading back toward the nation's capital. Vice President Dick Cheney was busy communicating with various agencies during the attacks from a bunker under the White House. He relayed a momentous message to the US Air Force. President Bush had ordered the shooting down of civilian aircraft that did not respond to commands from US fighter planes. But there were no more hijacked planes to shoot down.

Of the four hijacked aircraft, only Flight 93 was still in the air. When air traffic controllers contacted the plane, the lead hijacker told them they were headed back to the airport. "Uh, this is the captain," he said. "There is a bomb on board."[10] Like the other hijackers, he was trying to keep the crew calm and confuse those attempting to track the planes. The passengers of Flight 93, however, took things into their own hands. Possibly aware that terrorists had crashed the other planes (thanks to cell phone calls from friends and relatives), they rushed the hijackers. The cockpit flight recorder picked up one passenger saying "let's roll,"[11] and then recorded the sounds of a struggle.

> "The pictures of airplanes flying into buildings, fires burning, huge structures collapsing, have filled us with disbelief, terrible sadness, and a quiet, unyielding anger."[12]
>
> —US president George W. Bush.

The plane crashed in a field in Shanksville, Pennsylvania, a little after 10 a.m., killing the thirty-three passengers, seven crew members, and four hijackers. The passengers likely prevented the hijackers from ramming the plane into another high-profile target—quite possibly the White House or the Capitol. Either target would have been easily visible from the air, and either would have provided the same symbolic shock as the attacks on the Pentagon and World Trade Center.

A Search for Answers

On the evening of September 11 the US president addressed the nation from the White House. "The pictures of airplanes flying into buildings, fires burning, huge structures collapsing, have filled us with disbelief, terrible sadness, and a quiet, unyielding anger,"[12] Bush said.

Investigators search for the flight data recorder from the hijacked airliner that crashed in a Pennsylvania field on September 11, 2001. Experts suspect the plane was headed for the White House or Capitol Building.

As the shock began to recede, anger took over. Nineteen Middle Eastern hijackers had entered the United States and brought American life to a standstill in two principal cities, New York and Washington. They had caused the death of thousands of civilians going about their daily lives and left iconic buildings in smoldering ruin. Many Americans wondered just who these hijackers were and why they wanted to attack the United States.

Bush had made it clear that America was gearing up for war. But just how would the United States wage a war against individuals bent on terrorism? This would be a different war from wars past. For decades the United States had been locked in a struggle with the Soviet Union and Communist China for global dominance. Civilian and military leaders had grown accustomed to planning for combat with large armies controlled by national governments. The war against terrorism, however, would be much murkier. It was new territory, ranging across countries pitting a superpower against networks of secretive terrorists.

The first step that US leaders took was to uncover the extent of the international conspiracy to attack the United States on September . Intelligence agencies quickly identified the nineteen hijackers and an to trace their movements. But there was a deeper conspiracy at work. It involved the growing threat of Islamist terrorism—the use of violence by religious extremists to achieve political ends. Islamist terrorism was not new. US intelligence agencies had already been tracking an individual known to be funding terrorism. This was Osama bin Laden, and they suspected that his loosely organized terrorist organization, known as al Qaeda, was behind the attacks.

Bin Laden had already helped Islamic fighters, known as mujahideen, wage war against another superpower long before the attacks on September 11, 2001. The mujahideen's success in that struggle proved to be a major factor in the rise of terrorism against the United States.

CHAPTER TWO

How Did the Afghan-Soviet War Contribute to the Rise of Islamist Terrorism?

Discussion Questions

1. If the United States and the Soviet Union had not partici-pated in wars in countries such as Afghanistan and Vietnam, would the Cold War have ended any differently? Explain.
2. Do you think it is good foreign policy for a country to support the enemies of its enemies, as the United States did with the mujahideen? Why or why not?
3. Why do you think that religious extremism has arisen within the Muslim community?

The attacks on September 11, 2001, seemed incomprehensible to many Americans. Why would anyone want to fly a plane into a large commercial building, killing themselves and thousands of civilians going about their daily lives far removed from conflicts in the Middle East?

While the attacks can seem incomprehensible in their cruelty and suddenness, it is entirely possible to read back in modern history to understand the rise of terrorism and the roots of al Qaeda. Al Qaeda came to represent a new age of national security threat, sometimes called the Age of Terror. But what was new is the reach of Islamist militants and their willingness to strike far from the Middle East and Central Asia. Islamist militancy was not a new phenomenon at all. In the decades before September 11, 2001, it was limited mainly to the Middle East. But the wider international struggle, known as the Cold War, breathed new life into the Islamist movement.

A Global Rivalry

The Cold War was a global struggle between the United States and its allies on the one side and the Soviet Union and aligned Communist governments on the other side. The Americans and Soviets had been allies during World War II. They cooperated to defeat Nazi Germany, which threatened both the Soviets in Eastern Europe and American allies in Western Europe. But the cooperation between democratic governments and the Soviet Union was one of convenience. They needed each other to defeat Germany, but they shared little else in common.

This alliance, known as the "Grand Alliance," quickly unraveled after the war. "Whatever the Grand Alliance's triumphs in the spring of 1945," writes Cold War historian John Lewis Gaddis, "its success had always depended upon the pursuit of compatible military objectives by incompatible systems."[13]

The Soviet Union and the United States emerged from World War II as global superpowers with political systems hostile to each other. In the postwar years the two superpowers competed all over the globe to spread their own systems of government. Because both had nuclear weapons, they were hesitant to face each other in open conflict. The result was the Cold War—a global struggle that involved conflict in smaller countries where the Soviets and Americans tried to limit each other's influence.

During the Cold War the Americans and the Soviets clashed through proxies. These were smaller countries allied with one side or the other. By clashing in other countries, the superpowers avoided direct confrontations with each other. On the Korean Peninsula, for example, US troops supported anti-Communist South Korean troops against North Korean forces backed by Communist China and the Soviet Union from 1950 to 1953.

Two years after the Korean War resulted in a stalemate, the United States began military support for the forces of South Vietnam. The Soviets and Communist Chinese, on the other hand, supported the Communist Viet Minh forces in North Vietnam. In both Korea and Vietnam the Soviets put to the test the Cold War strategy of fighting by proxy. They also tried to claim an air of legitimacy by stating that they were trying to end the civil wars that were tearing the countries apart. "A particular advantage of this strategy was that it would not

A US warship fires on enemy targets during the Korean War. The United States and Soviet Union fought on opposite sides but did not directly engage each other during this Cold War conflict.

require direct Soviet involvement: the North Koreans and the Viet Minh would take the initiative, operating under the pretext of unifying their respective countries,"[14] writes Gaddis.

Soviet strategy was to draw in larger numbers of US forces into South Vietnam and let Communist Vietnamese troops wear them down over time. The Vietnam War, which lasted until 1975, saw the increasing involvement of US troops and a growing number of US casualties. The United States would later use the same strategy in supporting enemies of the Soviets in Afghanistan and wearing down their troops without direct American military involvement.

Jihad Against Communism

When the Soviet Union invaded Afghanistan in 1979 to support a weak Communist government in Kabul, the capital, the United States saw an opportunity to strike at the Soviets without directly involving US troops. Resistance to the Soviet invasion fell mainly to

In the mosaic of resistance leaders that fought the Soviets in Afghanistan from 1979 to 1989, none became as revered as Ahmad Shah Massoud. Because he operated in the Panjshir Valley in northern Afghanistan, he was largely cut off from the arms and money flowing through Pakistan to mujahideen commanders in southern Afghanistan. Massoud, a talented linguist, read deeply from the history of guerilla warfare. He armed his fighters largely by capturing weapons from Soviet military columns traveling south through the mountain highways near the Panjshir Valley toward the capital, Kabul.

The Soviets tried to crush Massoud repeatedly because he was threatening their supply lines. They never succeeded, and Massoud earned the nickname "lion of the Panjshir" for his cunning abilities as a guerilla commander. He later served as minister of defense in a post-Soviet government and as vice president of Afghanistan. Although a devout Muslim, Massoud rejected the religious fundamentalism of a new political movement known as the Taliban. The Taliban had established a government in Kabul in 1996.

In April 2001 Massoud addressed the European Parliament in Brussels, where he warned that al Qaeda militants were planning to attack the United States. On September 9, 2001, al Qaeda operatives posing as reporters detonated explosives hidden in a news camera, killing Massoud just two days before al Qaeda attacked the United States.

tribal leaders, often deeply religious, who saw communism as a threat to their traditional way of life. Although storied fighters, the Afghan rebels were poorly armed when compared to the Soviet forces.

Shortly after the Soviet invasion, Zbigniew Brzezinski, the national security adviser to US president Jimmy Carter, feared that aggressive Soviet tactics would soon crush the Afghan rebels. "We should not be too sanguine about Afghanistan becoming a Soviet Vietnam," he writes. "They have limited foreign support, in contrast to the enormous amount of arms that flowed to the Vietnamese from both the Soviet Union and China."[15]

The anti-Soviet fighters, however, had a potent formula to win support from outside of Afghanistan. The resistance fighters were known as mujahideen, meaning those engaged in a religious struggle called jihad. The mujahideen held a twin appeal to both anti-Communist Cold Warriors who hoped to prevent Soviet expansion and to Muslims who believed that the Communist invasion of a Muslim country was an affront to their religion. Perhaps the most significant of the early jihadist voices was that of Abdullah Azzam.

A Palestinian by birth, Azzam became disillusioned with Palestinian leaders trying to establish a Palestinian State in lands controlled by Israel. He turned from the secular nationalist struggle toward a broader religious struggle against non-Muslims. He studied traditional Islamic law, but he was attracted most of all by a violent interpretation not shared by most Muslims. His fiery rhetoric against infidels, or non-Muslims, rallied other angry young Muslims to a violent global struggle to rid Muslim countries of foreign interference.

When the Soviets invaded Afghanistan, Azzam appealed to Muslims everywhere to resist the Soviets. "Azzam was both the ideological godfather and the global recruiter par excellence of Muslims drawn to the Afghan jihad,"[16] according to Peter L. Bergen, a terrorism analyst. Support quickly poured in, and it arrived in two forms.

The first was the arrival of young, mostly Arab men who answered the call to jihad against the Soviet Union. Camps sprouted up on Afghanistan's southern border with Pakistan to arm and train the fighters. Known as the Afghan Arabs, these volunteers revived a sense of communal identity long absent from Muslim lands. They were idealists united in a common cause. "In Afghanistan was assembled the first truly global army of Islamic warriors—the Afghan Arabs," writes Fawaz A. Gerges, a scholar of Islamist extremism. "For a fleeting moment in Afghanistan, in the eyes of Islamists and Muslims alike, there existed a community of believers united in arms against infidel encroachment and aggression."[17]

> "In Afghanistan was assembled the first truly global army of Islamic warriors—the Afghan Arabs."[17]
>
> —Fawaz A. Gerges, a scholar of Islamist extremism.

To organize and fund the volunteers, the Afghan Arabs also needed financial support and organizers to raise and distribute donations from wealthy supporters of the jihad. The most notorious of the facilitators for the Afghan Arabs was Osama bin Laden. The son of one of Saudi

Arabia's richest construction magnates, Bin Laden arrived in Afghanistan in 1980 at the age of twenty-three. Bin Laden brought to the struggle skills that were much in demand. While others provided arms and military training, Bin Laden helped build the infrastructure for mujahideen bases. He brought with him to Afghanistan "hundreds of tons of construction machinery, bulldozers, loaders, dump trucks, and equipment for building trenches, which he put at the disposal of the mujahideen,"[18] according to Bergen.

> "Our ultimate goal is the withdrawal of Soviet troops from Afghanistan."[19]
>
> —Zbigniew Brzezinski, national security adviser to US president Jimmy Carter.

Bin Laden's experience in the family construction business, his fabulous wealth, and his contacts with wealthy Saudi businessmen allowed him to take on an important organizational role at an early age. With Azzam, Bin Laden created the Bureau of Services, an organization that helped channel money and volunteers onto the Afghan battlefield. While Bin Laden would later become America's most wanted fugitive and the most famous terrorist in the world, his goal of driving Soviet forces from Afghanistan was shared by the United States.

Strange Bedfellows

As support for the mujahideen poured into Afghanistan, the US government became increasingly enthusiastic about the possibility of striking at the Soviets through the mujahideen. Brzezinski quickly changed his assessment. He increasingly thought that US support for the mujahideen could result in a drawn-out campaign in Afghanistan that would be very costly for the Soviets, just as US military involvement in South Vietnam was very costly for the Americans.

Brzezinski was one of the most aggressive anti-Soviet voices in the Carter administration. He was born in Poland and fled when the Soviets took control of the country in the early days of World War II. As national security adviser to the president he tirelessly advocated ways to beat back Soviet influence wherever possible. And US policy was quickly shifting toward a more ambitious campaign against the Soviets. "Our ultimate goal is the withdrawal of Soviet troops from Afghanistan," he writes. "Even if this is not attainable, we should make Soviet involvement as costly as possible."[19]

Since the anti-Soviet jihad was being waged to rid Afghanistan of foreign influence, the United States disguised the origin of aid to the rebels. The mujahideen were no more willing to have US troops on Afghan soil than they were to have Soviet troops on the ground. But they were eager for the money and weapons that could be supplied by the United States. Through the US Central Intelligence Agency, the chief spy agency of the United States, the United States began to supply the mujahideen through Pakistan, where arms and supplies could be transported over the border into Afghanistan. America had effectively joined the jihad.

The Afghan tribesmen were legendary warriors. They were accustomed to fighting in the country's rugged mountains. They could move faster than the Soviet forces, and they adopted the tactics of guerilla warfare. They avoided direct attacks on Soviet strongholds. The Soviet

Afghan resistance fighters, or mujahideen, pose for a photographer in 1980 during the Afghan-Soviet War. The war offered the US government a chance to strike indirectly at the Soviets.

forces held most of the cities and airbases, but when they ventured out of these strongholds the mujahideen struck swiftly and then retreated into the mountains to plan their next attack.

While the Afghan tribesmen needed no training in mountain warfare, they were severely outgunned by the Soviets. Using tanks, artillery, and fighter jets, the Soviets pounded mujahideen positions whenever they could find them. Above all, the mujahideen fighters feared a type of Soviet gunship known as the Hind. These helicopters could hunt down small groups of mujahideen and unleash terrifying barrages of rockets and machine gun fire. At the beginning of the campaign many mujahideen had only antiquated rifles, some left over from World War I, and they relied on primitive explosive devices to try to stop Soviet movement on the roads.

Arming the Mujahideen

US covert support helped to change the equation. The CIA, through a program known as Operation Cyclone, bought weapons from around the world and shipped them through Pakistan to the mujahideen. Generally, CIA officers bought Soviet-made weapons to avoid the introduction of US weapons to the battlefield. This was to help hide US involvement. As these weapons reached the mujahideen, their successes mounted. Shoulder-fired rockets destroyed Soviet tanks, and heavy machine guns peppered pursuing Soviet forces after raids.

To counter these techniques, the Soviets dispatched Special Forces units, known as *Spetsnaz*. These soldiers adopted the guerrilla warfare tactics of the mujahideen and began inflicting heavy losses. A newspaper report from 1986 describes a surprise attack by the swift-moving Spetsnaz. "Rebel commanders who examined the demolished post after the Soviets left came to a startling conclusion," the *Los Angeles Times* reported. "The Soviet commandos had climbed the sheer cliff and attacked from behind."[20]

To counter increasingly successful Soviet techniques, the United States increased funding to the rebels and shipped new weapons. In particular, the CIA had been hunting for a weapon to counter the feared Soviet attack helicopters. They decided on the US-made Stinger shoulder-fired missile that could target aircraft by homing in on the heat from its engines. The Stinger was portable, accurate, easy to

The proud mountain fighters of Afghanistan have bedeviled foreign invaders from antiquity to modern times. The Khyber Pass, the traditional gateway between Pakistan and Afghanistan, is an area of soaring peaks and winding roads. Essential as a trade route, the pass could be a deadly killing ground when foreign armies attempted to breach this mountain pass. Ancient armies under Alexander the Great felt the sting of angry defenders in 323 BCE. Other ancient invaders were also repulsed.

In the nineteenth century the British Empire suffered one of the most stunning defeats in its history after British soldiers marched from British India into Afghanistan. Sensing treachery, the British Army attempted to retreat from Kabul to a British garrison in Jalalabad about 90 miles (145 km) away in the winter of 1842. Of the forty-five hundred British and Indian troops and twelve thousand nonmilitary personnel in the retreating caravan only a single man survived to ride into Jalalabad. This was William Brydon, a British army surgeon. In a painting titled *Remnants of an Army*, Lady Butler, a British painter who favored historical subjects, depicted Brydon on horseback, unsteady and alone, emerging out of the eerie Afghan landscape.

The destruction of foreign armies in Afghan history earned it the nickname "graveyard of empires." Bolstered by the defeat of Soviet forces in 1989, this reputation haunted US and allied forces when they invaded in 2001 in response to al Qaeda's terrorist attacks.

use, and deadly. "It was a turning point," writes George Crile in his book about Operation Cyclone. "According to the CIA's estimates, seven out of every ten times a mujahid fired a Stinger, a helicopter or airplane came down."[21]

With the help of American weapons and funding, a formerly weak and disorganized mujahideen resistance provided a real contest for the technologically advanced Soviet army. "In the jihad's early years," writes one scholar, "the two sides battled to a stalemate, but an influx of US funding and weapons after 1984 began to turn the tide."[22]

The Base Forms

In 1989 the Soviets withdrew from Afghanistan. They had suffered tremendous losses and gained nothing. The United States considered this a tremendous Cold War victory. Although the price of aid to the mujahideen had risen steadily, it was much less costly than a direct confrontation with the Soviets, and the campaign required no American troops.

The Soviet's failed war in Afghanistan contributed to momentous changes that were happening in Moscow, the Soviet capital. And in 1991, only two years after the campaign, the Soviet Union unraveled completely. The federation of states ruled by Communists in Moscow broke apart. The Cold War was over, and Americans celebrated their covert role in helping to destroy Soviet confidence on battlefields in Afghanistan.

Almost as soon as the Afghan campaign ended, however, US officials began to worry about the heavily armed Islamic fighters that they helped to create and arm. To take the Stinger missiles out of Afghan hands, the CIA began a buyback program to prevent the weapons from being used in terrorist attacks or military campaigns not supported by the United States. But only a limited number of Stingers were recovered. Some are thought to have remained in the hands of the Afghans, while some others were shipped to Iran, a nation the US government considers hostile to its interests in the Middle East. Many of the Stingers are still unaccounted for.

The United States also worried about the possibility that Islamic fighters, who had been hardened by a decade of war and violence, would turn against US allies in the Middle East, such as Saudi Arabia, Egypt, and Israel. Or, worse yet, the Islamic fighters might use their weapons and training to mount terrorist attacks on Western targets. Intelligence agencies call this phenomenon "blowback," which describes the unintended consequences of covert operations that end up causing harm in unforeseen ways.

After the Soviet withdrawal from Afghanistan, the Afghans for the most part were busy fighting for control of a nation ravaged by war. But the foreign fighters who fought alongside the Afghans debated the next step in their struggle to rid Muslim lands of foreign influence. Hardened by years of warfare away from home, these volunteers were emboldened by their role in the undreamed of victory over the Soviet superpower. "The question of what to do in the post-Soviet world was paramount among the fighters still in Afghanistan," writes one journalist. "One important line of thought came from the writings of Palestinian scholar and mujahid Abdullah Azzam, who in April 1988 wrote of the need for a 'pioneering vanguard' of Muslim warriors who would form the base, or 'qaeda,' of an Islamic society spanning the reaches of the long-lost Islamic empire that once stretched from the Philippines to Somalia, Eritrea and Spain."[23]

Azzam and Bin Laden formed al Qaeda in 1988, and unlike the Afghan jihadists they made it clear that their targets would lie beyond

> "The so-called United States will suffer the same fate as the Russians. Their state will collapse too."[24]
>
> —Osama bin Laden, leader of al Qaeda.

the Afghan battlefield. The United States did not fund Bin Laden and the Afghan Arabs during Operation Cyclone. But an unlikely alliance between American Cold Warriors and Islamic militants helped fuel the ambitions of those militants. Their success in Afghanistan stirred their ambitions to strike at enemies both near and far. "The so-called United States will suffer the same fate as the Russians," Bin Laden said. "Their state will collapse too."[24]

The Afghan-Soviet War was a training ground for foreign fighters. And after the war, their attention turned toward foreign targets all over the Middle East, and indeed all over the globe. Fighters trained in explosives and other military techniques set out to strike fear into other nations that, in their view, meddled in the politics of Muslim lands. Unlike in the Afghan war, however, their new campaign would target not just military enemies but also civilians in an attempt to intimidate foreign governments. This phenomenon—the growth of Islamist extremism—would radically change the nature of conflict in the decades that followed.

CHAPTER THREE

How Did Middle East Politics Contribute to the Rise of al Qaeda?

Discussion Questions

1. What role do you think colonialism played in stirring nationalism in the Middle East?
2. What are the main US interests in the Middle East? Why does it support the governments it supports?"
3. Why did terrorists target the United States when their primary grievances are governments in the Middle East?

The anti-Soviet campaign in Afghanistan fueled the ambitions of the Afghan Arabs. The choice of the name *al Qaeda* (the Base) indicates the organizers' intentions of creating a foundation for future operations. It is perhaps more useful, however, to think of al Qaeda as a network—a loose confederation of extremists representing different backgrounds and different grievances. A useful way to understand those grievances is to consider the nationalities of al Qaeda's founders. For although they agreed on the means of their struggle—the use of violence—each terrorist leader in the network was motivated by the historical narrative of his own home country.

Palestine

Abdullah Azzam, Bin Laden's mentor and one of the original founders of al Qaeda, began his journey into terrorism through his opposition to the founding of the State of Israel. The sliver of land running north along the eastern Mediterranean between Egypt's Sinai Peninsula and the tiny coastal nation of Lebanon has been marched over

Barbed wire placed on a main road separates Jews and Arabs in Jerusalem in May 1948, shortly after Great Britain partitioned Palestine into Jewish and Arab sections and Israel declared its independence as a Jewish state.

by armies from ancient times up to the present. The land is claimed as the ancestral home of both the Jewish people and the Palestinians. The Palestinians refer to the entire coastal strip by its ancient name, Palestine.

Despite their ancient heritage on the land, much of the Jewish population was driven from Palestine by successive waves of political violence beginning in the sixth century BCE. This resulted in the Jewish diaspora, the great fanning out of the Jewish people into other nations. Between the time of the ancient Jewish state, as recorded in the Bible, and the present day, Palestine was conquered by successive empires and used as a bridge between Egypt and other regions of the Middle East. The last empire that ruled the region was the Ottoman Empire, which governed from the Ottoman capital, Constantinople, which is today called Istanbul and is the capital of modern Turkey.

The Ottoman Empire dissolved after World War I, and the Ottoman Middle East was divided between the victorious European powers France and Great Britain. When the colonial powers finally withdrew, the British separated Palestine into Palestinian territory and Jewish territory. Because of the Nazi persecution of Jews in World War II, Jews flocked to Palestine, and in 1948 they declared the State of Israel on the Jewish portion of Palestine. Even at its founding, Israel was already at war with the Arab Palestinian population, which wanted the land for an independent state of its own.

While many nations refused to recognize the new country of Israel out of concern for alienating Muslims across the region, the United States became the first country to offer recognition and later became a major source of military support for the Israelis. "Arabs and Muslims in general feel deeply aggrieved over the plight of the Palestinians as well as outraged over American support for Israel," explains one Middle Eastern scholar. "Al Qaeda and other radical Islamist groups have sought to heighten as well as exploit these feelings in order to secure funding, recruits and sympathy from Arabs and other Muslims."[25]

The Palestinians to this day struggle for a country of their own. Those advocating for a Palestinian state fall into two distinct camps. On the one side are secular political organizations, such as the Palestine Liberation Organization, and on the other are religious groups, such as Islamic Jihad and Hamas. Disillusioned with the secular organizations, Abdullah Azzam became an influential voice in the religious camp. From a young age he was both scholarly and deeply devout. The 1967 Arab-Israeli war caused Azzam to flee Palestine and take up refuge in neighboring Jordan, as did so many other Palestinian refugees.

The struggle for a Palestinian national homeland motivated Azzam, but he became convinced that the Palestinian struggle should be tied to a greater Arab awakening that would drive all foreign forces out of the Middle East. In exile he became a radical Islamic preacher whose primary target was Israel's chief supporter, the United States. "He developed the idea that Muslims should fight one truly global

> "Arabs and Muslims in general feel deeply aggrieved over the plight of the Palestinians as well as outraged over American support for Israel."[25]
>
> —Mark N. Katz, Middle East scholar.

jihad against their enemies, first Russia and then America, rather than many narrow separate national fights against their immediate rulers,"[26] writes Bruce Riedel in the Daily Beast.

The State of Israel would ever after be on al Qaeda's enemy list, and US support for Israel became one of the justifications for jihad against America. But Israel was not the principal motivation of other senior al Qaeda members.

Egypt

Much of the radical religious philosophy that led to Islamist terrorism and the rise of al Qaeda flowed from Egypt. While Azzam is sometimes referred to as the "Father of Jihad," he had an Egyptian counterpart who was equally important in forming a set of beliefs for jihad. This was Sayyid Qutb, an educator and onetime employee of Egypt's Ministry of Education. The frail and scholarly Qutb was a prolific author who advocated for social justice before he turned to more violent ideas.

Egypt during Qutb's youth was ruled by Gamal Abdel Nasser, a former military officer, who became the leading advocate in the Middle East of cooperation among Arab states. Nasser was a secular nationalist for the Arab people, while Qutb felt deeply that only Islam could deliver the social justice that would lift Egyptians out of poverty and rid the country of military rulers. Qutb became a leading member of the Muslim Brotherhood, an Islamist organization. At first the Brotherhood welcomed Nasser's rule, since the military had rid the country of a king who was allied with the West. Qutb was angered, however, when Nasser turned against the Muslim Brotherhood. In 1954 Qutb helped the Muslim Brotherhood plan Nasser's assassination.

The plot was discovered, and Qutb and scores of other Islamists were imprisoned. In subsequent decades Egypt's Islamists advocated for the overthrow of the state. Egypt's prisons became a breeding ground for Islamist plotting. Qutb was hanged for his role in the plot to kill Nasser but not before his prolific writings provided jihadists with their intellectual justifications. "Qutb slid further toward militancy, formulating his distinctive brand of Islamism, which advocates violently toppling non-Islamic governments and replacing them with

The writings of Sayyid Qutb (1906–1966) are considered a primary source of political Islam and an inspiration to terrorist organizations such as al Qaeda. Qutb grew up in an Egypt rapidly becoming modern. He attended a British-style school, a lingering influence of the former colonial power that once ruled Egypt. Qutb wrote novels and loved the sound of the Koran, Islam's holy book. Although a Muslim for his whole life, Qutb was open to Western education in his early years and critical of schools that only taught the Koran.

He spent two years in the United States studying education. What he found in the United States, however, met with his disapproval. The United States was still a segregated country, and he felt prejudice as a person of color. He disapproved of student dances and the way that women dressed. Islamists argue that women should be covered and modest. He also disliked the violence of American sports, such as boxing and football. And he disapproved of the US government's support for Israel.

Although disdainful of life in America, Qutb's anger was directed at Egyptian society. He believed that only by returning to Islamic law could Egypt rid itself of corruption and achieve social justice. This combination of political aims and religious teachings became a model for Islamist extremists. Qutb was hanged in 1966 after plotting a failed assassination against Egypt's president, Gamal Abdel Nasser.

puritanical Muslim theocracies," according to one Middle East scholar. "His life and voluminous writings have inspired generations of terrorists."[27]

Chief among those inspired by Qutb was Ayman al-Zawahiri, who became the leader of al Qaeda after Bin Laden was killed in 2011. Trained as a surgeon, Zawahiri had joined the Muslim Brotherhood at the age of fourteen. He worshiped Qutb, and he embraced the same use of violence to rid Egypt of non-Islamist rulers. Eventually Zawahiri became a founding member of an even more radical group of violent jihadists, Islamic Jihad. In 1981 the organization achieved what Qutb had failed to do. It assassinated an Egyptian president, Anwar Sadat, Nasser's successor.

After an unsuccessful war against Israel, Sadat had signed a peace treaty with Israel in 1979. US president Jimmy Carter had brokered the historic deal between Sadat and Israel's leader, Menachem Begin. Egypt became the first Arab nation to recognize Israel as an independent country.

Sadat's peacemaking outraged Islamic Jihad, and Islamists in the military riddled Sadat with bullets during a military parade in Cairo, Egypt's capital. Zawahiri was arrested, and he claims to have been tortured in prison. The soft-spoken and scholarly Zawahiri became a chief advocate of terrorist attacks against Egypt's secular rulers after his release. In 1998 Zawahiri merged Islamic Jihad with al Qaeda. He was often described as the number two of the organization, but there is evidence that he guided Bin Laden's views on jihad. One Islamist in Zawahiri's group describes him as "bin Laden's mind."[28]

Inspired by Egyptian scholar Sayyid Qutb, Ayman al-Zawahiri (right) helped found the violent group Islamic Jihad. He later served as an adviser to Osama bin Laden (left) and became the leader of al Qaeda after Bin Laden was killed in 2011.

Egypt has always been the idea factory of the modern Middle East, and the struggle of Islamists in Egypt played an outsize role in shaping al Qaeda's goals. "While bin Laden is the public face and money bags of al-Qaeda, *all* its key members are Egyptian and *all* its ideology and tactics are based on Egyptian models,"[29] writes Peter L. Bergen before the death of Bin Laden.

Saudi Arabia

No matter what influence Zawahiri and other Egyptians had on al Qaeda, however, Bin Laden remained its leader. And for Bin Laden the primary target of the group would always be the government of Saudi Arabia and its close ally, the United States.

The Kingdom of Saudi Arabia plays a special role in the life of Muslims. Along its western stretches near the Red Sea sit the two most sacred cities in Islam—Mecca and Medina. Mecca is the birthplace of Muhammad, the religion's most important prophet. Muslims believe that Allah, the Muslim god, revealed to Muhammad the holy book of Islam, known as the Koran, in Mecca. Medina is Muhammad's final resting place. A pilgrimage to Mecca, known as the hajj, is a sacred duty for all Muslims. Saudi Arabia is a deeply religious country, and the care of the holy cities is an important obligation for the ruling family of Saudi Arabia, the house of Saud, which founded the modern state.

The ancient lands of Saudi Arabia became a modern nation only in 1932 when a desert sheik, or ruler, named Ibn Saud established a hereditary kingdom with the help of fundamentalist holy warriors. The discovery of oil in the desert kingdom made its ruling family fantastically wealthy. To help build the roads, mosques, and other buildings in a kingdom growing rich, the royal family relied on Mohammad bin Laden, an immigrant from Yemen, a nation bordering Saudi Arabia on the southern tip of the Arabian Peninsula. The riches accumulated by the Bin Laden family became a principal source of funding for the political causes of Mohammad's son, Osama bin Laden. While his father thrived in Saudi Arabia, his son

"While bin Laden is the public face and money bags of al-Qaeda, all its key members are Egyptian and *all* its ideology and tactics are based on Egyptian models."[29]

—Peter L. Bergen, terrorism scholar.

41

developed a hatred for both the Saudi royal family and its close relationship with the United States.

Alliance with the United States

The United States played a leading role in extracting Saudi Arabia's oil, which helped fuel the oil-thirsty US economy. In response to US support for the Israelis in the 1973 Arab-Israeli War, Saudi Arabia and other Middle Eastern oil producers temporarily cut off oil to the United States, causing the economy to slump and cars to line up outside gas stations in a scramble for dwindling gas supplies.

The US-Saudi relationship, however, was patched up under US president Ronald Reagan who enlisted Saudi Arabia in US efforts to limit Soviet power during the Cold War. During the Iranian Revolution of 1979, oil once again grew scarce as Iranian supplies were cut off. This time Saudi Arabia increased production by a million barrels a day to ensure that the United States did not run dry. In exchange, Washington authorized massive sales of US weapons to Saudi Arabia.

For Bin Laden, the Saudi royal family's close relationship with the United States represented an insult to Muslims. He believed that Saudi Arabia's leaders were no longer fit to govern Muslims. They had become rich, while many Saudis remained poor and jobless. "Millions of people suffer every day from poverty and deprivation," writes Bin Laden, "while millions of riyals [the Saudi currency] flow into the bank accounts of the royals who wield executive power."[30]

While Azzam focused on the Palestinian question and Zawahiri was fueled by anger at the Egyptian government, Bin Laden's first goal was the overthrow of the Saudi royal family. "Saudi Arabia's borders," writes journalist Steve Coll, "marked the reign of a single and illegitimate family, the al-Sauds, bin Laden argued."[31]

The corrupt and repressive governments in Egypt, Saudi Arabia, and in other parts of the Middle East became for al Qaeda the near enemy. Al Qaeda's leaders, however, became convinced that these governments could not be toppled unless the United States withdrew its military and financial support. Israel, Egypt, and Saudi Arabia are the most important of America's allies in the region. The terrorist group therefore held a particular hatred for the United States, which they referred to as the far enemy.

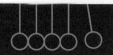

In 2010 citizens in many Middle Eastern countries took to the streets to protest repressive governments. For generations Arabs have had little choice in their own governance. Opposition was dangerous, and entrenched rulers were backed by their armies. The Arab Spring, as these uprisings are known, began in the tiny North African nation of Tunisia. When a fruit vendor named Mohammed Bouazizi wheeled a particularly good crop of fruit to the local market, a police officer tried to block him. The police had been preying on the market, stealing fruit and fining fruit sellers to line their own pockets.

Bouazizi resisted the police officer and later committed suicide as a protest against government corruption in Tunisia. His act of protest resulted in the toppling of Tunisia's dictator, who had ruled for twenty-three years. As protest movements spread from country to country, protesters demanded an end to corruption, greater democracy, and an end to police brutality. The rulers of Egypt, Libya, and Yemen were all pushed out of office. In other countries, such as Syria, the Arab Spring sparked civil war.

The Arab Spring represented a hopeful moment in Middle Eastern history. But these societies had little experience with democratic politics. Resistance to local dictatorships generally flowed from the mosque, the center of Muslim religious life. As a result, Islamists gained control briefly in Egypt and were emboldened elsewhere. Secular Arab Spring protesters were pushed aside. The one exception is Tunisia, where the protest of a fruit vendor resulted in the establishment of a moderate democratic government.

Declaration of War Against America

In 1990 Iraq invaded its Persian Gulf neighbor Kuwait. In response, the Saudi royal family asked the United States to deploy forces inside the kingdom to prevent Iraq from invading Saudi Arabia. This operation, known as Desert Shield, led to a massive buildup of American airpower and troops in Saudi Arabia. Bin Laden was outraged. The spectacle of US armed forces operating in the land of Mecca and Medina offended the religious sensibilities of Islamists.

Members of the US Army make their way through a line of concertina wire during a military exercise in the Saudi Arabian desert in 1990. Osama bin Laden was incensed that US armed forces were operating in Saudi Arabia during the Persian Gulf War.

Al Qaeda viewed this as a betrayal by the royal family. Although US forces were defending Saudi Arabia and in 1991 drove Iraqi troops out of Kuwait with the help of other Muslim nations, Bin Laden objected to the presence of US forces anywhere that Muslims lived. And while he despised Saddam Hussein, the dictator of Iraq, Bin Laden argued that only Muslims had the right to get rid of him. "It is true that Saddam is a thief and an apostate, but the solution is not to be found in moving the government of Iraq from a local thief to a foreign one," he writes. "Helping the infidel [Americans] to take the land of Muslims and control them is one of the ten acts contradictory to Islam."[32]

The First Gulf War (1991) drove Iraqi forces out of Kuwait but left Saddam Hussein in power. US forces stayed on in Saudi Arabia to protect the kingdom from another attack. In response, in 1996 Bin Laden called on the global community of Muslims, known as the *umma*, to wage jihad against the United States. "Men of the radiant future of our *umma* of Muhammad," he writes, "raise the banner of *jihad* up high against the Judeo-American alliance that has occupied the holy places of Islam."[33]

The terrorist cells of the al Qaeda network had already been conducting operations before Bin Laden's declaration of war. Plotters sought targets wherever opportunity presented itself. Some of the attacks were claimed by al Qaeda, and some are only suspected to be the work of the loosely organized group. For example, the month before Bin Laden's declaration a truck bomb exploded at the Khobar Towers in Saudi Arabia. The apartment complex was being used to house foreign troops. The bomb ripped the front off the building, killed nineteen Americans, and wounded another four hundred people.

On the morning of August 7, 1998, suicide bombers detonated explosives-laden trucks within minutes of each other at the US embassies in the East African nations of Kenya and Tanzania. The attacks killed 234 people, including 17 Americans, and injured thousands more. The attacks were traced to al Qaeda, and Bin Laden was placed on the FBI's Most Wanted List. The growing number of attacks awakened US authorities to the growing danger of al Qaeda.

Al Qaeda's leadership had long debated whether terrorist attacks should be limited to targets in the Middle East or whether the group should attack Americans on US soil. In 1993 Khalid Sheik Mohammad, a member of al Qaeda, orchestrated the first attack against the World Trade Center. A bomb-packed rented van was left in an underground parking lot. The explosion killed six people and wounded hundreds more. Although Bin Laden's involvement was uncertain, it is now known to be the work of al Qaeda. Bin Laden's war against America would culminate on September 11, 2001, when al Qaeda operatives turned American airliners into flying bombs and finished what they had started in 1993 by destroying the World Trade Center.

> "Raise the banner of *jihad* up high against the Judeo-American alliance that has occupied the holy places of Islam."[33]
>
> —Al Qaeda leader Osama bin Laden calling for war against the United States.

How Did the Attack by a Stateless Group Lead to US Wars in Afghanistan and Iraq?

Discussion Questions

1. Do you think that preemptive war is justifiable, as George W. Bush argued after the September 11 terrorist attacks?
2. Did the wars in Afghanistan and Iraq make Americans safer? Why or why not?
3. Should the United States and the international community use military power to topple governments that are oppressing their own people?

When Osama bin Laden declared war on the United States in 1996 from a hideout in Afghanistan, he was betting that his campaign of terror would drive the United States out of Muslim lands. "The perception that America was weak and could be driven out of the Middle East by feats of defiance and large-scale terror," writes journalist Patrick Tyler, "was becoming widespread."[34]

Bin Laden had already survived targeting by the US military, and he had only grown bolder in his war against America. After two car bombs ripped through US embassies in East Africa in 1998, President Bill Clinton authorized a direct strike against Bin Laden. US warships in the Arabian Sea released a barrage of cruise missiles targeting al Qaeda training camps in Afghanistan. It was hoped that the strike would take out Bin Laden and other leaders, but the camps proved to be mostly empty, and Bin Laden was unharmed. "He had been shot at by a high-tech superpower and the superpower missed," writes Steve Coll. "The missile strikes were his biggest publicity payoff to date."[35]

The problem of striking at a loosely organized terrorist group in the middle of an unfriendly country that was not at war with the United States bedeviled the White House. Al Qaeda's attacks on September 11, 2001, were so shocking to the American people that there was widespread support for a new approach. When President George W. Bush addressed a joint session of the US Congress nine days after the attacks, he outlined a new national security strategy. "From this day forward," he said, "any nation that continues to harbor or support terrorism will be regarded by the United States as a hostile regime."[36]

> "From this day forward any nation that continues to harbor or support terrorism will be regarded by the United States as a hostile regime."[36]
>
> —Former US president George W. Bush.

In the days after his declaration of war against terror, Bush demanded that the government of Afghanistan hand over Bin Laden

President George W. Bush receives a standing ovation during his address to a joint session of Congress nine days after the September 11 attacks. In his speech Bush outlined a new national security strategy and declared a US war on terror.

There has been no more effective military weapon in America's War on Terror than the unmanned aerial vehicle, more commonly known as a drone. The flying weapon requires no pilot and can penetrate unfriendly airspace from a distant command center. Drones have been used to decimate the leadership of terrorist organizations.

Their use, however, is highly controversial. The United Nations determined that their use violated international law because they represented targeted killings, essentially assassinations. Drones are also used in countries that are not at war with the United States. US drones have been used in Pakistan, Yemen, and Somalia while the United States was not at war with these nations. Drones can also miss their targets, killing civilians and prompting outrage among those who see US technology sowing fear into innocent populations.

President Obama rejected the doctrine, outlined by President George W. Bush after the September 11 attacks, of preemptive war against nations harboring terrorists. However, Obama has increased the use of drones to strike at terrorists and to avoid using US ground troops in large-scale operations.

and his associates. When the Afghan government refused, the United States put its new war doctrine into action. If Afghanistan's leaders would not hand over Bin Laden, then the United States would wage war on Afghanistan and hunt down the perpetrators of the terrorist attacks on America.

War in Afghanistan

By 2001 the Afghan civil war that broke out after the end of the Soviet occupation had been largely won by the Taliban, a group of Islamic fundamentalists who arose during the anti-Soviet campaign supported by the United States. The Taliban established the Islamic Emirate of Afghanistan and adopted a fundamentalist reading of Islamic law. They had much in common with Bin Laden, and life under the Taliban was terrifying for most Afghans. Thieves had their hands cut off as punishment.

People were flogged in public for minor infractions of their fundamentalist legal system. Music and dancing were outlawed. Women were banned from school and forced to cover up from head to toe. It was no surprise that they were unwilling to hand over Bin Laden, a fellow Islamist.

To topple the Taliban government and root out al Qaeda the United States rallied a formidable international coalition. The Bush White House was determined to go it alone if necessary, but the international community was also deeply shocked by the attacks on the United States. Among the casualties at the World Trade Center were more than five hundred people who had been born in other countries. The attack was widely seen as an attack on Western civilization itself.

The North Atlantic Treaty Organization (NATO), a military alliance designed to protect Western Europe from the Soviet Union, invoked Article 5 of the treaty, which considered an attack on any NATO member to be an attack on all the members. NATO allowed the United States access to military support from an allied coalition, though the US forces would largely lead the invasion. Far from being right about driving the United States out of Muslim lands, Bin Laden had awakened a sleeping giant now fully focused on the threat of terrorism.

Operation Enduring Freedom

In early October, less than two months after the attacks, US warplanes began to bomb Afghanistan in a campaign called Operation Enduring Freedom. They targeted air defenses and Taliban training camps. Special Forces from the United States and Great Britain linked up with a tribal coalition of Afghan fighters called the Northern Alliance. Although these fighters were Muslim warriors and anti-Soviet fighters, they rejected the Taliban's fundamentalist interpretation of Islam and remained independent of the Taliban government by force of arms. The beginning of the war presented the curious spectacle of Special Forces from the world's most sophisticated militaries riding on horseback with the Northern Alliance soldiers. The Special Forces soldiers helped coordinate the Northern Alliance forces on the ground and the NATO bombing missions raining destruction on the Taliban from the air.

The militaries of the United States and its coalition partners that invaded Afghanistan possessed some of the most sophisticated weapons in the world. They were aligned against an army of individualistic guerrilla fighters, who possessed few modern weapons and operated in a nation that had been ravaged by war for decades. Ferocious US bombing campaigns soon caused the Taliban frontline positions around Kabul to collapse, allowing Northern Alliance fighters to take the city. The victory had been remarkably swift, but it was only the beginning.

Like so many earlier invaders, the coalition forces were left fighting pockets of resistance in nearly impassable mountain ranges and towns and villages where the fighters mingled with the local population. As coalition forces spread throughout the country, they encountered fierce resistance from the Taliban and from al Qaeda's foreign fighters.

Foiled at Tora Bora

By December, however, US intelligence believed that Bin Laden was in a mountainous region on the border of Pakistan called Tora Bora, or the Black Cave. The area was a warren of caves and rugged mountains that had once been used as a base to fight the Soviets. US bombers attempted to smash the dug-in enemy from the air, while US and British Special Forces and allied Afghan tribes pursued bin Laden. In a lull in the fighting, Bin Laden and other al Qaeda members slipped across the mountains into Pakistan.

Bush's plan to destroy or capture al Qaeda by toppling the Afghan government that protected them had not worked out as planned. A month earlier Bin Laden had given a speech to local tribal leaders in which he "promised that they could teach the Americans a lesson, 'the same one we taught the Russians.'"[37]

While the United States had lost the leadership of al Qaeda to sanctuaries in Pakistan, the country was at least free of the Taliban in the major cities. The United Nations (UN) backed the establishment of a new government in Afghanistan, and more than forty countries contributed personnel to the International Security Assistance Force (ISAF) to keep order in the capital and protect the new government. For the most part the Afghan people were happy to see the Taliban driven out of power. Some danced in the streets for the first time in years. Girls returned to school as the harshness of life under the Taliban was swept away.

In November 2001 Taliban fighters (pictured) prepare for battle against US forces and US allies, including a coalition of Afghan warriors who rejected the Taliban's fundamentalist interpretation of Islam. Taliban fighters put up fierce resistance.

Yet, Bin Laden's prediction about teaching the Americans a lesson also proved true. Taliban and al Qaeda fighters continued to launch attacks from across the border. They waged guerilla warfare in the same manner as the mujahideen had fought the Soviets and often from the same bases in Pakistan. Although the Bush administration pressed Pakistan to do more to stop the militants from crossing the border, the country was unwilling or unable to put an end to the cross-border war. Nor was the United States about to invade Pakistan, a US ally armed with nuclear weapons. And so coalition forces settled in for what was to become America's longest war. US combat operations ended only in 2014, with a large contingent of US troops remaining in Afghanistan to support a government that is still battling the Taliban.

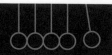

In 2014 President Barack Obama announced that the US military would conduct an air campaign to bomb a group of radical Islamist terrorists that had spread out from Syria into Iraq. The announcement made Obama the fourth US president in a row to order an air campaign over Iraq. Obama has been a reluctant warrior. He views the long-term solution to terrorism as one of changing attitudes and the slow building of peaceful institutions in the region. Warfare is conducive to neither.

But the Islamic State in Iraq and Syria (ISIS) demonstrates the lingering dangers of Islamic terrorism. The group is so violent that al Qaeda is reported to have rejected its widespread use of violence against Muslims. The group threatens the stability of Iraq, which the United States spent nearly a decade fighting for. It also highlights the difficulty for a US president to forgo the use of military force when confronted with a growing threat from a terrorist group.

The War in Iraq

Despite the early disappointment of failing to capture Bin Laden in Afghanistan, Bush doubled down on his strategy of attacking countries that could pose a future threat to the United States. Bush's father, former US president George H.W. Bush, had waged war on Iraq to drive Saddam Hussein out of Kuwait and to protect Saudi Arabia, a US ally. As president, his son considered Saddam Hussein a lingering threat. British and American intelligence agencies believed that Saddam Hussein still possessed biological and chemical weapons and was perhaps pursuing nuclear capabilities. Arguments were also made that Iraq had connections to al Qaeda.

In his 2002 State of the Union address delivered to the US Congress and televised for the American public, Bush described the case against Iraq. "Iraq continues to flaunt its hostility toward America and to support terror," Bush argued. "States like [Iraq], and their terrorist allies, constitute an axis of evil, arming to threaten the peace of the world."[38]

The US Air Force was at that time flying missions over Iraq to prevent Saddam Hussein from bombing his own population. Inspectors from the UN were also searching for chemical and biological weapons and finding nothing. The UN remained skeptical of a new war, but Bush received backing from the US Congress and the support of Great Britain, America's closest military ally, and a few other nations.

The United States launched a ferocious barrage of airstrikes on Iraq and then launched a ground invasion northward from Kuwait toward Baghdad, the capital of Iraq, in March 2003. While US and British fighter jets pounded targets around the country, the invasion force smashed through lines of Iraqi tanks and frontline troops guarding the approach to the capital. In three weeks US forces entered Baghdad, effectively ending the regime of Saddam Hussein, who had caused trouble for American presidents for over a decade.

The United States and its allies had performed marvelously in the initial invasion. America was good at destroying large armies. But as the skeptical world watched in the aftermath of the invasion, the United States could find no evidence that Saddam Hussein was harboring weapons of mass destruction—biological, chemical, or nuclear weapons. Iraq's supposed weapons programs along with possible links to al Qaeda were the main reasons that the Bush administration had declared war. Moreover, the connection to al Qaeda was also later disproved. Iraq played no role in the September 11, 2001, attacks on the United States.

When the reasons for invading Iraq proved to be flawed, dissent quickly grew at home. Richard N. Haass, an American official who helped plan the First Gulf War that drove Saddam Hussein out of Kuwait, summarizes the growing doubt over America's arguments for invading Iraq. "My bottom line is that it was still objectively a war of choice," he argues. "It was not a war that needed to be started at the time."[39]

The Iraq War did much to discredit Bush's strategy of preemptive war that he had outlined after the September 11 attacks. International law specified that countries could legally defend themselves only if

> "States like [Iraq], and their terrorist allies, constitute an axis of evil, arming to threaten the peace of the world."[38]
>
> —Then US president George W. Bush.

attacked. The international community rallied in support of the invasion of Afghanistan because the terrorist attacks of 2001 were traced directly to terrorists in Afghanistan.

But Iraq was a different case. Evidence that Iraq posed an immediate threat to the United States evaporated, though many American and British officials believed there was evidence at the time. "Defeating Saddam was conflated with bringing war to the terrorists," writes former US vice president Al Gore, "even though it really meant diverting attention and resources from those who actually attacked us."[40]

Of more immediate concern, however, was the rise of an insurgency in Iraq akin to the ongoing guerrilla warfare against NATO troops in Afghanistan. When it toppled Saddam Hussein the US military disbanded the Iraqi army. Many of the commanders joined with militants who opposed US forces in Iraq. These militants were later joined by al Qaeda operatives from abroad and by local Islamic extremists. While many Iraqis were glad to be rid of Saddam Hussein, the US invasion stirred up another problem. "As violence surged in occupied Iraq," according to the *Atlantic Monthly* correspondent James Fallows, "the International Institute for Strategic Studies in London reported that al-Qaeda was galvanized by the wars in Afghanistan and Iraq."[41]

It was like kicking a hornet's nest, and US troops would spend the next eight years trying to establish a peaceful, friendly government in Baghdad while battling a widespread insurgency. The US military fought on in Iraq until 2011, when the campaign was officially ended.

New Strategies

The wars in Afghanistan and Iraq were the principal military responses to the terrorist attacks on the United States in 2001. The United States military proved itself extremely skilled at defeating enemy armies and toppling governments. But the presence of US ground troops in Muslim countries proved to be a constant source of resentment and fueled insurgencies in both countries. Osama bin Laden had miscalculated when he believed that terrorist attacks would drive US forces out of the Middle East. But the invasions stirred a deep resentment over US policy toward Muslim countries.

US soldiers storm a regional government office building in Iraq in 2003. The United States and its allies launched air strikes and a ground invasion that ended the regime of Saddam Hussein.

Although the United States was fighting in defense of the Arab nations of Kuwait and Saudi Arabia during the First Gulf War and defending Muslims from the brutality of the Taliban in Afghanistan, it was creating the impression that the United States was constantly waging war against Muslims. There were also suspicions in the Middle East that the United States was primarily interested in obtaining access to the oil supplies located in Saudi Arabia, Kuwait, and Iraq.

These were the same claims made by Bin Laden in his opposition to the alliance between Saudi Arabia and the United States. "Those claims are that the United States will travel far to suppress Muslims, that it will occupy their holy sites, that it will oppose the rise of Islamic governments, and it will take their resources,"[42] explains Fallows.

Both US presidents George W. Bush and his successor, Barack Obama, have repeatedly emphasized that the United States is not at war with Islam. "We respect your faith," said Bush to Muslims around the world. "It's practiced freely by many millions of Americans, and by millions more in countries that America counts as friends. Its teachings are good and peaceful."[43]

President Obama, who was elected in 2008 on an antiwar platform, addressed the Muslim world from the Egyptian capital, Cairo, as one of his early acts as president. "As a student of history, I also know civilization's debt to Islam," he said. "I have come here to seek a new beginning between the United States and Muslims around the world; one based upon mutual interest and mutual respect."[44]

The US military response to the September 11 attacks was ferocious. And the United States has not suffered another major attack since. But the United States is still struggling both to improve relations with the Muslim world and to deprive terrorists of support from angry Muslims hardened by decades of war. In the end it was not America's war in Afghanistan or Iraq that led to the killing of al Qaeda's leader.

> "I have come here to seek a new beginning between the United States and Muslims around the world; one based upon mutual interest and mutual respect."[44]
>
> —US president Barack Obama speaking in Cairo.

In May 2011, nearly ten years after the terrorist attacks, US intelligence had tracked Bin Laden to a compound in Pakistan. A helicopter raid was launched, and American Special Forces burst into his compound, shooting their way through his guards. Bin Laden was killed in the raid and subsequently buried at sea so that his resting place could never become a shrine for Islamic extremists.

By the time of his death, however, al Qaeda had already splintered, and new terrorist threats were emerging in the Muslim world. America's wars in Muslim lands reinforced the idea that defeating terrorism would not come from military power alone.

CHAPTER FIVE

How Did Life in the United States Change After the September 11 Attacks?

Discussion Questions

1. Did the September 11 terrorist attacks succeed in making American society more fearful? Explain your answer.
2. Should the US government be allowed to monitor phone and e-mail communications to help uncover terrorist plots? Explain your answer.
3. Do you think news organizations should have the right to reveal secret government programs to the public? Why or why or not?

The terrorist attacks on September 11, 2001, came as a shock to an America long used to being safe from the dangers of the world. With the exception of the 1941 attack on Pearl Harbor, Hawaii, and the Cold War, when Americans worried about a nuclear missile attack from the Soviet Union, the United States had always enjoyed a particular sense of security. The country is bounded on the east by the Atlantic Ocean and on the west by the Pacific Ocean. Friendly neighbors, Canada and Mexico, share borders to the north and to the south. During most of America's wars, the fighting took place on foreign battlefields, oceans away and with little risk to America's citizens at home.

When the hijackers turned routine flights into terrifying weapons of destruction, that sense of safety vanished. "The theme that comes through repeatedly for me is that 9/11 changed everything," Vice President Dick Cheney said on the two-year anniversary of the attacks.

"It changed the way we think about threats to the United States. It changed our recognition of our vulnerabilities."[45]

Immediately after the attacks Americans were struggling to understand those new vulnerabilities. And in those first few weeks, one of the most noticeable changes was the change in the public mood. Americans exhibited a shared sense of purpose and unity rarely seen in the hodgepodge of regional and ethnic identities, class differences, and political partisanship. "New York became a small town immediately after 9/11," reports one life-long New Yorker. "It was New York in a way I'd never seen it. There was no more stranger danger. We all knew we better support each other."[46]

> "New York became a small town immediately after 9/11."[46]
>
> —Julia Torres Barden, New York City resident.

In sprawling New York, America's most populous city, crime had always been a chief safety concern. The city had gotten a little safer during the years just before the attack, but no one was prepared for what happened just after the terrorist attack. Even as the police were focused on search and rescue near the World Trade Center, ever since called Ground Zero, New York remained remarkably calm. "Despite a sputtering economy and a police force preoccupied with search and rescue operations, crime did not shoot up in the streets of New York City during the month following the devastating attacks on the World Trade Center," writes one journalist. "Violent crime, in fact, went down."[47]

Protecting the Homeland

While average citizens showed a remarkable ability to get their lives going again after the terrorist attacks, the federal government was scrambling to ensure that no other attacks would reach America's shores. A host of agencies contributed to America's domestic security in a piecemeal fashion. The Immigration and Naturalization Service facilitated the process of becoming a new American, and the US Border Patrol attempted to keep illegal immigrants out of the United States. Airports were protected by private companies hired by the airlines. These agencies largely worked independently of each other.

The federal government decided that a new strategy was needed. The agencies were going to have to coordinate their efforts to prevent terrorists from easily crossing US borders and passing unsuspected through US airports, as they did prior to September 11. In his address to Congress just after the attacks Bush announced the creation of a new agency, the Department of Homeland Security. The head of the agency sat on the president's Cabinet, which includes most senior advisers to the president. The new agency, formed in 2002, took over responsibility for immigration, border protection, and passenger screenings at airports.

In the wake of the attacks, airport security shifted to the newly created Transportation and Security Administration (TSA), which is part of the Department of Homeland Security. In place of private contractors, airline passengers would now be screened by federal employees with rigorous new guidelines, and airports would use all sorts of new equipment. Aside from new baggage scanners, there were people

Airline passengers remove their shoes as they go through security checks, including metal detectors, at Chicago's O'Hare Airport. New airport screening procedures enacted after the September 11 attacks have resulted in long lines and added scrutiny at airports.

Color-Coded Fear

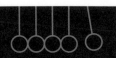

In the months after the September 11 attacks the Department of Homeland Security created the Homeland Security Advisory System, which was more commonly known as the terror alert level. One of five colors—red, orange, yellow, blue, and green—indicated the probability of a terrorist attack taking place in the United States. Red indicated the highest probability of an attack; green represented the lowest threat level.

The system triggered responses from federal authorities, placing them on higher alert, generally accompanied by greater security measures. From the first year of the new system, in 2002, until the system was replaced in 2011, the terrorist threat level never fell below yellow, which indicated an elevated threat. Changes in the threat level at first prompted anxiety in Americans. A 2009 review by the Department of Homeland Security found that the alert system offered the public little useful information. Other critics noted that the threat levels rarely corresponded to attacks, with more of them occurring when it was yellow than when it was elevated to orange or red.

Over time, people simply ignored the alert system, since they had little to do in response and were growing increasingly skeptical of its accuracy. "A terrorist threat level that warns of a 'significant risk of terrorist attacks'— that's what yellow is—for years is ignored," writes Bruce Schneier, who works on security technology.

Bruce Schneier, "Why Terrorist Alert Codes Never Made Sense," CNN.com, January 28, 2011. www.cnn.com.

scanners that could look beneath clothing to detect bombs or weapons. New rules also required the removal of shoes and belts.

The screening procedures took time, and lines lengthened at security checkpoints. Travelers were routinely singled out for additional screening, and stories of the elderly, children, and the handicapped being treated like terrorism suspects made news headlines. When a TSA agent patted down a seven-year-old girl with cerebral palsy, for example, a British newspaper interviewed the outraged parents. "She's not a threat to national security," her father said. "They treat her like she's Osama bin Laden."[48]

Increasingly, people questioned whether these methods were really making America safer from another terrorist attack. TSA argued repeatedly that the measures were helping, but many were skeptical and increasingly annoyed at being manhandled during security screenings and treated like suspects while traveling in their own country.

Bruce Schneier, a security specialist, describes this as security theater, or a show of security to make people feel safer. "When people are scared, they need something done that will make them feel safe, even if it doesn't truly make them safer," Schneier writes about the airport security policies after September 11. "Politicians naturally want to do something in response to crisis, even if that something doesn't make any sense."[49]

Suspicion of Others

In the years after the terrorist attacks Americans struggled to find the right balance between protecting themselves from another terrorist attack and giving up the freedoms that they held so dear. In New York citizens were asked to become the eyes and ears of the police. The New York subway system was decorated with a new catch phrase urging awareness—"If you see something, say something."

The catch phrase became an emblem of changed life in America after September 11. It was eventually adopted by the Department of Homeland Security. The intention, of course, was to involve the millions of eyes and ears of the American people to help stop a future terrorist attack. But an unfortunate result of the campaign was an increase in suspicion. "The phrase has been criticized by many for fueling paranoia and fear," reports the *New York Times*.[50]

> "When people are scared, they need something done that will make them feel safe, even if it doesn't truly make them safer."[49]
>
> —Bruce Schneier, specialist in security technology.

Of particular concern were suspicions falling on Arab Americans and others mistaken for Muslim terrorists. People with olive skin and dark hair or who wore traditional clothing from the Middle East or

South Asia were sometimes assumed to be a threat to national security. This phenomenon is known as profiling, or singling out people for investigation based on observable characteristics or expressions of religious beliefs. "Whenever anyone is targeted due to their perceived physical appearance, faith, or nationality," says the author of a post–September 11 study on the effects on minority groups, "we all become potential targets."[51]

The government, too, was trying to balance the historical openness of American society against the need to protect Americans from another terrorist attack. Immediately after the attacks immigration became a heated topic of debate. The attackers had all entered the country legally, and investigators wanted to know how to prevent others from using legal immigration as a cover for terrorist activities.

Detaining Immigrants

Hundreds of immigrants were detained as a result. For the most part they were detained because they had stayed too long on a visa or had come illegally into the country. "Since September 11, 2001, the federal government has relied heavily on immigration law and policy to prosecute the so-called 'War on Terror,'" explains a 2011 report on human rights published by the New York University School of Law. "With fewer checks and balances, it is much easier for the government to arrest, detain, and investigate an individual under immigration law than criminal law."[52]

Since the attackers were all Muslim extremists, suspicion fell most heavily on the Middle Eastern immigrants. "An Egyptian antiques dealer from Arkansas named Hady Hassan Omar made plane reservations on a Kinko's computer around the same time one of the hijackers did so at the same place; he spent two months in jail before being released," reported the *New York Times* in November 2001.[53]

Immigration law was not previously used in quite the same manner. The detentions of specific groups of people on immigration violations, which are extremely common in a nation of immigrants, raised concerns that an entire group of people was being punished for the actions of the terrorists. There is some precedent for this in US history. During World War II, for example, people of Japanese ancestry were detained due to fears that they would side with Japan, which the US was at war with. In 2007 three descendants of interned Japanese Americans campaigned on behalf of Muslims against a court ruling in New York that defended the government's targeting of the group. "The ruling 'painfully resurrects the long-discredited legal theory' that was used to put their grandparents behind barbed wire, along with the rest of the West Coast's Japanese alien population,"[54] reports the *New York Times*.

The use of immigration policy to prevent terrorism was often challenged in the courts. And challenges to the legality of these policies sometimes reached the Supreme Court, the highest appeals court in the country, which determines whether laws violate the Constitution, America's most fundamental legal document.

Justice Anthony M. Kennedy, one of the nine justices of the US Supreme Court, noted the harmful impact on the Muslim community in a decision upholding the use of immigration policy to fight terrorism. "It should come as no surprise," he writes, "that a legitimate policy directing law enforcement to arrest and detain individuals because of their suspected link to the attacks should produce a disparate, incidental impact on Arab Muslims, even though the purpose of the policy was to target neither Arabs nor Muslims."[55]

> "It should come as no surprise that a legitimate policy directing law enforcement to arrest and detain individuals because of their suspected link to the attacks should produce a disparate, incidental impact on Arab Muslims."[55]
>
> —Supreme Court Justice Anthony M. Kennedy.

Civil Liberties

Just as some immigrants and law-abiding Arab Americans were made uneasy by the government's new approach to fighting terrorism, so too were those worried about the government's expanded powers to monitor citizens within the United States. Civil liberties are a central legal concept in American life. These are the guarantees that are afforded to citizens by the Constitution, such as the right to due process—a legal protection that guarantees a fair trial and protects citizens from being detained by the government without cause.

In an attempt to make Americans safer after the September 11 terrorist attacks, the US Congress passed the USA Patriot Act. The law expands the powers of law enforcement agencies to better detect terrorist activities. The law, for example, makes it easier for the government to follow suspects and to listen in on their phones or search their computers. "Existing law was written in the era of rotary telephones," President George W. Bush said at the signing ceremony. "This new law that I sign today will allow surveillance of all communications used by terrorists, including e-mails, the Internet and cell phones."[56]

Of fundamental importance was the authorization for law enforcement agencies to gather intelligence through wiretapping or surveillance of suspects within the United States. This effectively eroded the traditional barrier against domestic spying. While US intelligence agencies spy on people in other countries, they are generally not allowed to spy on Americans at home unless a judge has been shown evidence for probable cause.

The Patriot Act was passed with strong support from both Democrats and Republicans on October 26, 2001. It was later learned that few lawmakers had read the entire bill before voting on it. Many of the new rules made people uncomfortable. In response to the terrorist threat, Americans were essentially giving their government more power to pry into their lives. The measures were strongly criticized by civil liberties advocates, who viewed the expansion of government power as a threat to individual freedoms with little benefit in combating terrorism. "The national security benefit of all these measures is questionable,"[57] writes one critic of the Patriot Act.

Even the law's sponsor, Jim Sensenbrenner, a Republican member of the House of Representatives, opposed the way it was used to invade the privacy of American citizens by the National Security Agency (NSA), a federal intelligence agency that uses technology to spy on foreign targets. "What the NSA has done, with the concurrence of both the Bush and Obama administrations, is completely forgotten about the guarantees of civil liberties that those of us who helped write the Patriot Act in 2001 and the reauthorization in 2005 and 2006 had written the law to prevent from happening,"[58] he said in a 2013 interview with the *Washington Post*.

A book store in Seattle, Washington, takes part in a petition drive protesting the possibility of government access to bookstore and library records under the Patriot Act. The Patriot Act gave law enforcement new powers to fight terrorism but also raised many privacy concerns.

The global war on terror that George W. Bush announced in the days after the September 11 attacks presented some thorny legal questions. How exactly were terrorism suspects supposed to be tried for their crimes? The United States guarantees legal protections for those accused of a crime to receive a fair trial, including a legal defense team and the right of appeal.

To avoid giving terrorism suspects these rights, the US government decided to imprison them at a military facility in Guantánamo Bay on the island of Cuba. The detainees were classified as enemy combatants and denied trials in civilian courts. The American government did not want terrorists to use American courts as a platform to spread their ideas. It was decided that terrorism suspects would be tried in military tribunals, or courts, which offer lesser protections than civilian courts. The question of a fair trial for the suspects was further muddied by revelations that some prisoners had been subjected to "enhanced interrogation techniques," which many Americans considered torture.

After being elected president in 2008 Barack Obama ended these practices and ordered the facility shut. The problem, however, was what to do with the prisoners. The US Senate blocked a plan to transfer them to prisons in the United States. Neutral countries were sought out to take released detainees, and some have been transferred. But the prison remains open to this day.

Balancing Liberty and Security

At the root of the problem was the question of how to prevent terrorism. Law enforcement generally responds to crimes after they are committed. Police can only respond to a robbery, for instance, after it has taken place. The Patriot Act and other laws intended to fight terrorism, however, were intended to prevent a crime before it happened. Americans did not want to wait until they were attacked again to stop the terrorists.

Much like Bush's idea of preemptive war—to strike first at nations that might threaten the United States—the Patriot Act was designed to give law enforcement the tools to detect terrorist plots before they happened. This involved watching and listening to suspects in a way that challenged civil liberties that are protected by Constitution. The rights of individuals were bumping up against the government's desire to expand its powers to prevent terrorism. Perhaps the greatest bombshell in the debate over domestic spying arrived in 2013 when a young former intelligence contractor named Edward Snowden revealed secret surveillance programs to the media.

Edward Snowden speaks via a 2014 teleconference in Austin, Texas. Snowden revealed to several major media outlets a variety of secret government programs, including government efforts to monitor phone and e-mail records of American citizens and foreign governments.

In the wake of September 11, US and foreign intelligence agencies had been trying to harness technology to try to prevent terrorist attacks. The documents that Snowden gave to the media indicated that the NSA had been scooping up the phone and e-mail records of American citizens. "One program, code-named PRISM," reports the *Washington Post*, a newspaper that received some of the stolen documents, "extracts content stored in user accounts at Yahoo, Microsoft, Facebook, Google and five other leading Internet companies."[59]

The government surveillance of e-mail accounts and phone records represented a challenge to individuals' privacy and to the rights of private companies to operate without government interference. The companies that provide phone service and e-mail accounts naturally worried that they would lose customers if their role in the spying programs was publicized. The government in effect was recruiting private companies to act secretly in the war against terrorism.

Phone records, text messages, and e-mails were also being picked up unintentionally in huge numbers. In some cases intelligence agencies were simply looking for patterns that could be used to detect possible plots, but the legal questions over domestic spying are still being hashed out in the courts. Lawmakers are also trying to write laws that both prevent terrorism and ensure legal protections for privacy.

> "I think it's important to recognize that you can't have 100 percent security and also then have 100 percent privacy and zero inconvenience."[60]
>
> —US president Barack Obama.

American leaders have the difficult task of seeking the right balance, one that will reassure Americans about security and privacy while still affording them protection from terrorist acts. "When I came into this office, I made two commitments that are more important than any commitment I made: Number one, to keep the American people safe; and number two, to uphold the Constitution. And that includes what I consider to be a constitutional right to privacy and an observance of civil liberties," Obama said in a June 2013 speech after the news of the domestic spying program came to light. "But I think it's important to recognize that you can't have 100 percent security and also then have 100 percent privacy and zero inconvenience. We're going to have to make some choices as a society."[60]

Introduction: Understanding the Unthinkable

1. Franklin Delano Roosevelt, "A Date That Will Live in Infamy" Speech, audio recording, US National Archives, December 8, 1941. www.archives.gov.
2. John Lewis Gaddis, "And Now This: Lessons from the Old Era for the New One," in *The Age of Terror: America and the World After September 11*, ed. Strobe Talbott and Nayan Chanda. New York: Basic Books, 2001, p. 6.
3. Gal Luft and Anne Korin, "Terrorism Goes to Sea," *Foreign Affairs*, November/December 2004. www.foreignaffairs.com.
4. Michael Lind, "The World Is Actually More Peaceful than Ever," *Salon*, April 23, 2013. www.salon.com.
5. Gaddis, "And Now This," p. 9.

Chapter One: A Brief History of the September 11 Attacks

6. Quoted in *New York Times*, "The 9/11 Tapes: The Story in the Air," audiotape and transcript, September 7, 2011. www.nytimes.com.
7. Quoted in *New York Times*, "The 9/11 Tapes: The Story in the Air."
8. Stephen Evans, "Ground Zero," in *The BBC Reports on America, Its Allies and Enemies, and the Counterattack on Terrorism*. New York: Overlook, 2002, p. 22.
9. World Trade Center, "Fire, Part 2," FDNY 911 Telephone Calls, transcript, September 11, 2001, p. 16. http://content.ny1.com.
10. National Commission on Terrorist Attacks Upon the United States, *The 9/11 Commission Report: The Final Report of the National Commission on Terrorist Attacks on the United States*. New York: Norton, 2004, p. 29.
11. NBC News.com, "United Airlines Flight 93 Cockpit Tape Transcript." www.nbcnews.com.
12. George W. Bush, "Statement by President George W. Bush in His Address to the Nation," 9/11 Primary Sources, 9/11 Memorial. www.911memorial.org.

Chapter Two: How Did the Afghan-Soviet War Contribute to the Rise of Islamist Terrorism?

13. John Lewis Gaddis, *The Cold War: A New History*. New York: Penguin, 2005, p. 6.
14. Gaddis, *The Cold War*, p. 42.
15. Quoted in Steve Coll, *Ghost Wars: The Secret History of the CIA, Afghanistan, and Bin Laden, from the Soviet Invasion to September 10, 2001*. New York: Penguin, 2004, p. 51.
16. Peter L. Bergen, *Holy War, Inc.: Inside the Secret World of Osama bin Laden*. New York: Free Press, 2001, p.51.
17. Fawaz A. Gerges, *Journey of the Jihadist: Inside Muslim Militancy*. Orlando, FL: Harcourt, 2006, p. 111.
18. Bergen, *Holy War, Inc.*, pp. 50–51.
19. Quoted in Coll, *Ghost Wars*, p. 51.
20. Rone Tempest, "Afghan Rebels Face Tougher Foe in Elite Soviet Commando Units," *Los Angeles Times*, May 24, 1986. http://articles.latimes.com.
21. George Crile, *Charlie Wilson's War: The Extraordinary Story of How the Wildest Man in Congress and a Rogue CIA Agent Changed the History of Our Times*. New York: Grove, 2003, p. 437.
22. Anand Gopal, "How the Soviet-Afghan War Made the Taliban," Vice.com, September 23, 2014. www.vice.com.
23. Jamie Tarabay, "How the Afghan Jihad Went Global," Al Jazeera, November 12, 2013. http://america.aljazeera.com.
24. National Commission on Terrorist Attacks Upon the United States, *The 9/11 Commission Report*, p. 123.

Chapter Three: How Did Middle East Politics Contribute to the Rise of al Qaeda?

25. Mark N. Katz, "The Israeli-Palestinian Conflict and the War on Terror," Middle East Policy Council, December 20, 2010. www.mepc.org.
26. Bruce Riedel, "The 9/11 Attacks' Spiritual Father," Daily Beast, September 11, 2011. www.thedailybeast.com.
27. Eric Trager, "A Dangerous Mind," *Wall Street Journal*, July 17, 2013. http://online.wsj.com.
28. Quoted in Bergen, *Holy War, Inc.*, p. 203.

29. Bergen, *Holy War, Inc*, p. 199.

30. Quoted in Bruce Lawrence, ed., *Osama bin Laden, Messages to the World: The Statements of Osama bin Laden*. New York: Verso, 2005, p. 247.

31. Coll, *Ghost Wars*, p. 270.

32. Quoted in Lawrence, *Osama bin Laden*, p. 255.

33. Quoted in Lawrence, *Osama bin Laden*, p. 29.

Chapter Four: How Did the Attack by a Stateless Group Lead to US Wars in Afghanistan and Iraq?

34. Patrick Tyler, *A World of Trouble: The White House and the Middle East—from the Cold War to the War on Terror*. New York: Farrar, Straus and Giroux, 2009, p. 467.

35. Coll, *Ghost Wars*, p. 412.

36. George W. Bush, "Address to the Joint Session of the 107th Congress," *Selected Speeches of President George W. Bush, 2001–2008*, p. 69. http://georgewbush-whitehouse.archives.gov.

37. Quoted in Seth G. Jones, *In the Graveyard of Empires: America's War in Afghanistan*. New York: W.W. Norton, 2010, p. 97.

38. George W. Bush, "President Delivers the State of the Union," White House Archives, January 29, 2002. http://georgewbush -whitehouse.archives.gov.

39. Richard N. Haass, "The Iraq Invasion 10 Years Later: A Wrong War," *Huffington Post*, March 15, 2013. www.huffingtonpost.com.

40. Al Gore, *The Assault on Reason*. New York: Penguin, 2007, p. 38.

41. James Fallows, *Blind into Baghdad: America's War in Iraq*. New York: Vintage, p. 144.

42. Fallows, *Blind into Baghdad*, p. 145.

43. Bush, "Address to the Joint Session of the 107th Congress."

44. Quoted in *New York Times*, "Text: Obama's Speech in Cairo," June 4, 2009. www.nytimes.com.

Chapter Five: How Did Life in the United States Change After the September 11 Attacks?

45. Quoted in NBC News, "Transcript for September 14," *Meet the Press*. www.nbcnews.com.

46. Quoted in Sarah Ottney, "Eyewitness: 'New York Became a Small Town After 9/11,'" *Toledo Free Press*, September 11, 2001. www .toledofreepress.com.

47. Sandip Roy, "NYC Crime Drops Post-9/11—a Blip or a Trend?," *Pacific News Service*, November 7, 2001. http://news.newamerica media.org.

48. Beth Stebner, "'They Treat Her Like She's Osama bin Laden': Family's Outrage as TSA Pats Down Their Daughter, SEVEN, Who Is Mentally Handicapped and Has Cerebral Palsy," *Mail-Online*, April 25, 2012. www.dailymail.co.uk.

49. Bruce Schneier, "Is Aviation Security Mostly for Show?," CNN.com, December 29, 2009. http://edition.cnn.com.

50. Manny Fernandez, "A Phrase for Safety After 9/11 Goes Global," *New York Times*, May 10, 2010. www.nytimes.com.

51. Quoted in Amna Nawaz, "Thirteen Years After 9/11, Report Finds a Community Under Attack," NBCNews.com, September 9, 2014. www.nbcnews.com.

52. Center for Human Rights and Global Justice, Asian American Legal Defense and Education Fund, *Under the Radar: Muslims Deported, Detained, and Denied on Unsubstantiated Terrorism Allegations*. New York: NYU School of Law, 2011, p. 3.

53. Jodi Wilgoren, "Swept Up in a Dragnet, Hundreds Sit in Custody and Ask, 'Why?,'" *New York Times*, November 25, 2001. www.nytimes.com.

54. Nina Bernstein, "Relatives of Interned Japanese-Americans Side with Muslims," *New York Times*, April 3, 2007. www.nytimes.com.

55. Quoted in Adam Liptak, "Civil Liberties Today," *New York Times*, September 7, 2011. www.nytimes.com.

56. George W. Bush, "Text: Bush Signs Anti-Terrorism Legislation," *Washington Post*, October 25, 2001. www.washingtonpost.com.

57. Louise Cainkar, "The Impact of the September 11 Attacks on Arab and Muslim Communities in the United States," in *Maze of Fear*, ed. John Tirman. New York: New Press, 2004, p. 216.

58. Andrea Peterson, "Patriot Act Author: 'There Has Been a Failure of Oversight,'" *Washington Post*, October 11, 2013. www.washingtonpost.com.

59. Barton Gellman, Julie Tate, and Ashkan Soltani, "In NSA-Intercepted Data, Those Not Targeted Far Outnumber the Foreigners Who Are," *Washington Post*, July 5, 2014. www.washingtonpost.com.

60. Barack Obama, "Statement by the President," Office of the Press Secretary, the White House, June 7, 2013. www.whitehouse.gov.

Books

Karen Armstrong, *Islam: A Short History*. New York: Modern Library, 2007.

Moustafa Bayoumi, *How Does It Feel to Be a Problem? Being Young and Arab in America*. New York: Penguin, 2009.

Wendy Biddle, *Immigrants Rights After 9/11*. New York: Chelsea House, 2008.

Julia Clancy-Smith and Charles Smith, *The Modern Middle East and North Africa: A History in Documents*. New York: Oxford University Press, 2013.

Editors of *Salon*, *Afterwords: Stories and Reports from 9/11 and Beyond*. New York: Washington Square, 2002.

Dean E. Murphy, *September 11: An Oral History*. New York: Doubleday, 2002.

David Rose, *Guantanamo: The War on Human Rights*. New York: New Press, 2004.

Malala Yousafzai and Patricia McCormick, *I Am Malala: How One Girl Stood Up for Education and Changed the World*. Boston: Little, Brown, 2014.

Websites

40 Maps that Explain the Middle East (www.vox.com/a/maps-explain-the-middle-east). A creative look at Middle Eastern history from ancient times to the present using maps.

9/11 Attacks (www.history.com/topics/9-11-attacks). An interactive timeline and video archive of events on September 11 by the History Channel.

9/11 Memorial Oral Histories (www.911memorial.org/oral-histories-0). Audio files of witnesses, first responders, and others recalling the events of September 11.

The September 11 Digital Archive (http://911digitalarchive.org). A digital collection of photographs and audio recordings related to the events of September 11.

Spying on the Home Front (www.pbs.org/wgbh/pages/frontline /homefront/). Acclaimed PBS series *Frontline* examines the rise of domestic spying in the wake of September 11.

"What Were the Causes of 9/11?" (www.prospectmagazine.co.uk /features/whatwerethecausesof911). Terrorism expert Peter Bergen examines some of the theories that help explain the motivations of the September 11 attackers.

INDEX

Robert Green writes about the politics of Hong Kong and Taiwan for the Economist Intelligence Unit. He holds a master's degree in journalism from New York University and a master's degree in area studies from Harvard University. He witnessed the collapse of the Twin Towers from the Brooklyn Promenade, which sits just across the water from lower Manhattan.